The Halo Resting on Your Brow

The Halo Resting on Your Brow

A Marriage Guide to Building a Love That Heals

Sandy Haney

Novelle Publishing, LLC

Copyright © 2026 Sandy Haney

All rights reserved.

ISBN: 978-1-967131-08-2

The Halo Resting on Your Brow

No part of this book may be reproduced without written permission of the author; nor may any part of this work be reproduced, stored in a retrieval system, transmitted in any form or by any means, electrical, mechanical, photocopying, recording, or otherwise, without the prior permission of the author. All recommendations are made without guarantee on the part of the author or publisher. The author and publisher disclaim any liability in connection with the use of this information.

Scripture quotations are taken from the Holy Bible, New Living Translation, copyright © 1996, 2004, 2015 by Tyndale House Foundation. Used by permission of Tyndale House Publishers, Inc., Carol Stream, Illinois 60188. All rights reserved.

This book is not meant to diagnose, treat, or advise on any legal, psychological, or medical matters. Readers are encouraged to seek professional help or counseling when needed. The publisher and author disclaim any liability for any loss or damage incurred as a direct or indirect result of the content of this book.

Novelle Publishing, LLC

CONTENTS

Introduction To The Halo Resting On Your Brow 5

Acknowledgements 9

Chapter One – Patience: Slowing Down To Grow Together 11

Chapter Two – Kindness: Choosing Gentle Words And Actions 25

Chapter Three – Contentment: Guarding Against Envy 46

Chapter Four – Humility: Letting Go Of The Need To Impress 57

Chapter Five – Surrendered Pride: Walking In Mutual Respect 73

Chapter Six – Honoring Your Spouse: Lifting Each Other Up 87

Chapter Seven – Selflessness: The Joy Of Putting Us Before Me 99

Chapter Eight – Calm Spirit: Responding Instead Of Reacting 114

Chapter Nine – Forgiveness: Clearing The Ledger 127

Chapter Ten – Integrity: Loving What Is Good 144

Chapter Eleven – Protection: Creating A Safe Haven 164

Chapter Twelve – Trust And Hope: Anchoring In God's Faithfulness 180

Chapter Thirteen – Perseverance: Holding On When It's Hard 196

Conclusion: Halos And Healing – Loving Through It All 209

Introduction to The Halo Resting on Your Brow

More than four decades later, he still knows how to take my breath away. Our kids used to ask me how I knew he was the one I should marry. I shared how my elderly babysitter taught me from a young age to choose for my husband a man who loved God with all his heart, like no one I'd ever met before, and how that man was him. Laughter doubled me over when he and I first met because of his dry humor, delivered with that adorable southern accent, and he still knows how to make me giggle.

I knew that marrying him was the right thing because my heart felt like it would break for the month we were apart, 1,500 miles apart, during Christmas vacation from Bible college. I slept with his glistening senior ring on my finger, a dapper picture of him under my pillow, and an unmistakable love for him in my heart. Those are the things a little girl's dreams are made of, and they came at a time when I thought the fulfillment of dreams was for everyone else but me.

That Valentine's Day, he proposed, and that summer, we were married. Like Ruth, I vowed, "Wherever you go, I will go; wherever you live, I will live. Your people will be my people, and your God will be my God (Ruth 1:16b)."

If you are like me, or if your spouse is like me, you understand what it is to have the pain of the past complicate the already-challenging struggles of marriage. Let's tackle that issue head on together in this guide. I realize my husband and I have so much farther to go in learning to be the couple God would have us to be, so much room left in our figurative treasure chest for pearls of wisdom. However, I honestly believe God can use our insight to spare you unnecessary grief. Herein lies our gems, pearls of wisdom harvested while maturing in Christ together.

There are times when the last thing I want to hear from my husband is how much more proficiently he can accomplish a task than I can, and he lets me know that the same is true of him. I'm especially sensitive to his criticism because of my past. As a result, I lose my temper as I struggle under the weight of my many roles. His heart becomes hardened toward me, and he refuses to be supportive of me. We hit an impasse, rebelling against being the union God has called us to be. In those moments, I catch myself staring at what feels like a halo resting on his brow. It isn't a genuine straightened symbol of godliness in which grace and comfort are being extended and we are drawing closer to the Lord, but a tilted sarcastic one of superiority that provokes frustration and distances us from our Savior. Only God can soften my heart enough to remind me of the man I married and his incredible heart for the Father. I repentantly fall to my knees in prayer for my husband, for us, and await our crowns to come.

At the risk of inundating the opening paragraphs with metaphorical idioms, let's deal with the elephant in the room right off the bat. A wife's submission and a husband's respect will filter through the pages of the guide. Ephesians 5:22-27 receives more criticism than any other Bible passage on marriage. I've heard people complain that the passage is outdated, that it reflects a time when women were nothing more than property. You're not going to believe this, but after typing the preceding sentence, I turned on the televised newscast, to a conservative channel, no less, and there sat a panel of women discussing this very controversy. I get that this is a hot-button issue for women. However, I personally know abuse all too well, and my volunteer work with the abused further showed me its ugliness. I would never teach you wives to be its victim.

As you move through these pages, you will come to understand that I submit to my husband and he cherishes me because we find pleasure in doing so. When I honor his headship of the home, that takes his breath away and makes it easy for him to be a team player. When he cherishes me, that makes it easy for me to care for him. When he honors me and treats me with understanding (1 Peter 3:7), his chivalry vacuums every liter of breath from my being. We are not abusive of each other. In fact, there are triggers of past wounds and insecurities that we recognize and choose *not* to engage in, out of compassion for the spouse that is still healing. We lovingly show patience for each other and trust God's timing rather than reacting impulsively. Examine Philippians 2:1-2 and see how He instructs us to accomplish this.

This guide contains thirteen marriage principles, in honor of 1 Corinthians 13—often referred to as the Bible's love chapter. Each principle includes:
- Personal examples from our journey (though not in chronological order),
- Biblical couples or references,
- A teaching-focused elaboration on the principle,
- Reflective questions to guide further study, and
- Trauma teaching tools and exercises.

The reflection questions at the end of each chapter in this guide are for your contemplation. They don't require you to write your responses, but you may if you choose. They are meant to open the doors of communication and introspection. The trauma teaching tools and exercises included in this guide aim to teach you how the Love quality (Example: Perseverance) influences the traumatized spouse and increases faith. It explains the reaction the traumatized spouse may have when attempting the Love quality (Example: Exhaustion). It reiterates the chapter's teaching but from the standpoint of trauma. The tools and exercises help you actively engage in improving your marriage. There are tips for the supporting spouse, too. (Example: You are not responsible for healing what you did not break, but you are called to stand beside your partner in faith. Leave your spouse a note of encouragement.)

This guide can be used as a resource for couples, group Bible studies, premarital or marital counseling, or other types of counseling. You'll find moments of levity, tenderness, and the music of words. It's our prayer not only to grow as a couple in Christ, but that you, too, will grow in Him as you read our story.

Acknowledgements

First and foremost, I wish to thank my Lord and Savior, Jesus Christ. The thought that He would have such sacrificial love for someone like me still brings me to my knees. Thank you, Lord, for your example.

My father-in-law, a preacher, was married to my mother-in-law for 62 years before his passing. Marty and I spent almost all of our marriage nearby, learning from their example what a Christian marriage looks like. I'm thankful for their example, and I hope this book honors my father-in-law's memory.

To our kids; thank you for your tolerance as your dad and I practiced in front of you. Marriage can be difficult in the best of circumstances, let alone when a spouse suffers from past trauma. Thank you for kneeling with us under the double rainbow as kids, for your understanding and forgiveness, and for committing your own marriages to God as adults. We love you and your dream-come-true spouses so, and we are very proud of you.

To our grandkids, when Paw Paw asks for some sugar to stir into the tea, thank you for allowing Nanny to kiss him in front of you! We love our four snuggle bugs like crazy!

To our pastor and his wife, we so appreciate you pouring into our marriage, and your encouragement toward this project.

To Donna and Brandie, thank you for your strengths where I was weak concerning this book, and for the countless hours you gave it.

Finally, thank you to the man who still knows how to take my breath away. You looked upon this girl with such compassion all those many years ago. You found something beautiful beneath my rubble, and you chose me for your wife. Your most tender love for God made me fall in love with you then, and it still does to this day. Your unending patience with the painful things seared into my memory is your endearing quality. I know how you hate attention. Thank you for letting me write this book anyway for the cause of Christ. You are my dream come true.

Chapter One – Patience: Slowing Down to Grow Together

Patience is one of the clearest reflections of God's love in a marriage. Scripture reminds us in 1 Corinthians 13:4 "Love is patient," setting the standard that patience is not passive waiting but a deliberate act of love. In marriage, it shows up in the moments when tempers flare, when expectations are unmet, or when life simply feels overwhelming. Choosing patience means choosing to pause, to listen, and to trust God's timing rather than rushing to have our own way. As we begin this chapter, I want to invite you to see patience as a spiritual practice—one that makes room for grace, protects unity, and allows both you and your spouse the space to grow together in love.

The Basics of Being Together

In Philippians 2:1-2, Paul says, "Is there any encouragement from belonging to Christ? Any comfort from his love? Any fellowship together in the Spirit? Are your hearts tender and compassionate? Then make me truly happy by agreeing wholeheartedly with each other, loving one another, and working together with one mind and purpose."

Though Paul was addressing the body of believers and not spouses, the basics of being together are still the same. If your spouse is oddly on the defensive, there may be more to the sacred cow than meets the eye. Be compassionate with your spouse by being sensitive to the things that haven't healed, and by demonstrating patience until they have. Love each other and work toward the same goal, glorifying God.

Practical Examples of Patience: The Laundry for Me, A Halo for Him

Marty and I have been married for forty-four years at the time of this writing. We've learned the sacred cows, those things we hold that are not to be criticized, in each other's lives. One of mine is laundry. Even when I was pregnant, I got up early to do the laundry. I pretty well kept it done up as our kids grew, and if it piled up, I went to the laundromat to knock it out in one fell swoop. I pride myself in keeping us looking presentable, right down to our dogs' blankets. For these reasons, if I should have an off week and fall behind on our laundry, the last remark I want to hear from Marty is, "You haven't finished the laundry yet? I was able to do all of mine in one day while you were gone!"

Typically, such a remark receives a glare as I ponder the halo resting on his brow. Once the remark is followed by an article of clothing he finds stains on from his improper washing, I feel justified in ensuring the laundry is done well, no matter how long it takes.

Pillow-Like for Me, Marble-Like for Him

The more time you spend together, the more you learn the sacred cows of your spouse. Just as the laundry is my sacred cow, the cooking is Marty's. I was raised on Bisquick dumplings, which inflate to large fluffy pillows in the broth. Marty prefers small, marble-like drops of dough from scratch. The Bisquick dumplings are to be left unstirred in the broth until cooked, while Marty's dumplings are stirred frequently to ensure their small size. If I criticize Marty's dumplings, I might not get any for a very long time, as he is the chief cook in our home. Each occasion that I'm tempted to say, "You could defeat Goliath with these dumplings," I remember when I've offended him before and went for a while without his good cooking.

When Patience is Missing

In those moments when we see a trigger set off and we don't demonstrate love's patience with our spouse, the argument that ensues is often about what's behind that trigger, not what's in front of us. When we stop and think about how an argument is formed, we can see where patience is lacking.

The Anatomy of an Argument

One of Marty's sacred cows, as you recall, is the cooking. He felt disrespected in front of company. My reasons for not doing things his way were rational, but I ignored his feelings. When he felt disrespected and ignored, he saw the halo tilted on my brow. When he didn't want to listen to my reasons, I felt my intelligence being insulted, and I saw the halo tilted on his brow.

After company left, we talked about our feelings. That's not as easy as it may sound. Marty was raised by a dear man who had to support his preacher's income with carpentry. My father-in-law was notorious for analyzing what needed to be done and doing it, with very little conversation along the way. Thus, Marty takes the same approach to life. I have to patiently coax him to do more than grunt like a caveman and to actually give his feelings words, which is what I did when company left the day of our argument.

Likewise, I tend to shut down when I start feeling unwanted, stupid, and destined for failure. It's like pulling a half-ton pickup by hand trying to get me to speak. The quarrel may have been over trivial matters and quite silly, all in all, but today's little snowballs of hurt feelings become tomorrow's avalanche. Finally, we were able to start identifying the triggers. Marty apologized and agreed to be more patient as I heal from past wounds. I apologized and agreed to be more sensitive to his need to be respected and acknowledged.

Patience in Crisis: An Impasse in Our Marriage

When our kids were young, Marty and I hit an impasse in our marriage. There seemed to be no feasible solution to our problem, and we couldn't see any way around divorce. … Marty didn't understand my continued struggle with childhood trauma, and I didn't know how to effectively communicate it. Combine that with frustrations in child-rearing, which is challenging for the best of us, and the culmination is an impasse.

The Double Rainbow

We gathered up the kids and drove ninety miles to a hotel to get away for a bit and clear our heads. I didn't mind that it was raining as we piled into the van. No one could distinguish my tears from the raindrops. The storm on the outside was synonymous with the storm in our family. Once inside the hotel, I walked over to the enormous picture window and shoved the drapes apart. The most glorious and vivid double rainbow stole my breath… We all stood there, eventually wrapping ourselves in each other's arms with tear-drenched faces.

The second bow in a double rainbow is a mirror image of the first. Its colors are exactly the same as the first bow's colors, but in reverse order. What a metaphor for the approach we should take in living for God as a couple. We should strive together to be a mirror image of Him.

No matter the feelings we feel at that impasse, the right thing to do is to practice patience with each other, and patience to wait on God as He reveals His encouragement to us. Sometimes feelings in the moment are deceiving, and having patience through those feelings to wait on God and wait on our spouse is what we need to do.

We knelt right then and there and prayed (and cried) as a family. We talked about the significance of the double rainbow. We knew God would see us through our struggle. When it was time to return home, we knew we would be okay. We discussed that God is faithful to keep His promises. He did not reject our repentant hearts (Psalm 51:17). Because we remained faithful to Him and to each other, He was faithful to us (Psalm 18:25). Because we put patience into practice and waited on God instead of rushing toward divorce, He held us together. *"Those who wait on the Lord will renew their strength. They will soar on wings like eagles, they shall run and not be weary, they shall walk and not faint."* (Isaiah 40:31 NKJV) We committed to show patience with each other by having more open lines of loving communication. This made all the difference in our home.

Byproducts of a Painful Past

Consider that sometimes the sacred cows represent the deeper things within the soul. They are byproducts of a painful past. One of my sacred cows used to be my intelligence. If I thought Marty was insulting it, I lashed out with my tongue like a prize fighter meaning to win. "I'm not stupid, you know," I ranted. "I was shown to have an IQ in the superior intelligence range. You don't have to talk to me like I have no intelligence whatsoever."

The truth is that when I was a girl, the grandmother who raised me sent mixed signals. She told others how smart I was, but at home she ridiculed me for doing "stupid" things. (She was a result of her own painful past.) Thus, as an adult, if I felt anyone was disrespecting my intelligence, I came out fighting. Herein lies the importance of considering that there might be something deeper going on with your spouse than just a sacred cow.

Marty never talks about his school-age years. He had a very loving home, but he experienced heartache at school. Once I realized he hated being disrespected because it reminded him of those painful years, I understood that trigger.

To identify these triggers or sacred cows with your spouse, have an open conversation when both of you feel safe, not in the middle of an argument. Have the discussion when you can both be honest and not defensive and have it out of love. This will require a lot of patience for the non-traumatized spouse. That is why LOVE is PATIENT. We have to see the wound and not condemn the wounded. Healing takes time and love and patience.

Summary

I always thought life would be like a late 1970's love song. While it was the sweet things a teenage girl's dreams are made of, life is much more complicated than the answer to all our problems being our spouse. That title belongs to God. Learning to submit to Him makes it easier to submit to Marty. Submission is not outdated. I can trust that God will forever only have my best interest at heart, and that He will help Marty learn to do the same.

Leave the sacred cows alone. Look past the halo resting on your spouse's brow. Let your spouse know that his or her contribution to the home is valued. Each spouse has a valuable contribution to the relationship despite the cows or triggers that they carry. It is our duty when we make that commitment to understand those triggers don't disappear overnight or after one discussion. Patience is continuous. It is the key to managing those sacred cows. Remember that sacred cows can be byproducts of a painful past and be compassionate. God will use your struggles for good. He wants your marriage to thrive. We need to wait on God's promises even when things are hard. Have patience with one another and wait on God as He will renew you.

Chapter One Questions:

Reflect on the questions below about how you demonstrate (or don't demonstrate) patience in your marriage. Use the space provided to capture your thoughts. Discuss them with your spouse if you both agree.

When you read that "Love is patient, love is kind" (1 Corinthians 13:4), what does patience look like in your marriage in daily, ordinary moments?

Philippians 2:1-2 calls believers to be "tender and compassionate." How might applying this to your marriage change the way you approach disagreements?

Do you see patience as a spiritual practice? How would your marriage be different if you treated it as an act of worship to God rather than just self-control?

What are some "sacred cows" in your life—areas where you are most easily triggered or defensive?

How do you typically respond when your spouse unknowingly steps on one of those sacred cows?

What might it look like to pause and extend patience in those moments rather than reacting?

The text says, "Today's little snowballs of hurt feelings become tomorrow's avalanche." What small habits in your marriage could grow into bigger problems if patience is missing?

When was the last time you felt disrespected or misunderstood? How could patience have changed the outcome of that moment?

How does your spouse's background (family, upbringing, past wounds) shape the way they handle conflict—and how might recognizing that help you show more patience?

In what situations do you personally find it hardest to be patient with your spouse? Why do you think that is?

Do you tend to rush to "fix" things, or can you wait on God's timing in your marriage struggles?

What fears or insecurities from your own past make patience harder for you?

How can patience be a tool for healing wounds from past trauma within your marriage?

What steps could you and your spouse take to create safe spaces for honest, non-defensive conversations about triggers?

Looking back at the story of the double rainbow, how has God reminded you of His promises during seasons where patience was required?

Trauma Awareness: Patience

Every marriage has its "sacred cows"—the unspoken places where a spouse feels tender or easily provoked. In trauma-affected marriages, these sacred cows often manifest as *hot buttons* that stem from past abuse, neglect, or betrayal. They are not stubborn quirks to be "fixed," but protective reflexes shaped by painful experiences. When a survivor reacts strongly, it is rarely about the present moment alone, rather than an old wound being touched.

For this reason, patience in marriage is not optional; it is the very soil in which healing grows. Scripture reminds us, *"Be completely humble and gentle; be patient, bearing with one another in love"* (Ephesians 4:2). Bearing with one another means slowing down, noticing what lies beneath the reaction, and choosing compassion over correction.

As you engage these tools, remember that they are not about proving who is right or wrong. They are about learning to recognize where fear hides in your spouse's heart and offering gentleness that says, *"You are safe with me."* When you discover your spouse's triggers, don't treat them as weaknesses to criticize but as invitations to love more intentionally. If you are the **supporting spouse**, pay special attention to the **Trauma Support Application** notes attached to each activity. They show you how to use tone, timing, and gentle actions to help your partner feel at ease and talk through both of your feelings.

Patience doesn't mean ignoring problems or pretending the hurt isn't there. It means creating space for God's Spirit to work in both of you. As Proverbs 19:11 says, "A person's wisdom yields patience; it is to one's glory to overlook an offense." Patience in this sense is wisdom that chooses healing over hurry.

Below you will find tools and exercises designed to help you as a couple identify sacred cows, understand their deeper roots, and respond with patience that builds safety and trust.

Tool: Trigger Spotting

- **Step 1:** Individually—This week, make a list of situations or words that tend to set you off. Pay attention to moments when your reaction feels stronger than the situation warrants. Focus on what triggered you, not the reaction itself.
- **Step 2:** Prayerfully—Ask God to show you where these "hot buttons" come from. Many trace back to painful past experiences.
- **Step 3:** Together—Share 1 or 2 items from your list with your spouse. This is not a time for correction, but for compassion. Listen carefully to each other's vulnerabilities.

"Search me, O God, and know my heart; test me and know my anxious thoughts. Point out anything in me that offends you, and lead me along the path of everlasting life."(Psalm 139:23–24)

Journal about one trigger you identified. What memory or feeling might be beneath it? Invite God to bring healing there.

Exercise: Pause and Pray Before Responding

- **Step 1:** Agree on a plan: Before tackling sensitive topics, decide together that either of you may call a "Pause."
- **Step 2:** Use a 3-step pause: (1) Stop the argument, (2) Take a few deep breaths, (3) Pray together, even briefly.
- **Step 3:** Resume with grace: After prayer, return to the conversation with patience and gentleness. Remind each other that your commitment is to understanding, not to "winning."

"Everyone should be quick to listen, slow to speak and slow to become angry." (James 1:19)

At the end of the week, ask: When did pausing help us avoid an argument? How did praying together change the tone of our discussion?

Trauma Support Application

As the supportive spouse, resist the urge to minimize or fix. Simply listen, nod, and affirm what you hear. Encourage your partner that you can be trusted with their story by being a calm presence. This helps create safety and makes it easier for your spouse to be honest. Sometimes, you need to be the one to gently suggest the pause when you sense emotions rising. Lead the prayer with a short, simple line—*"Lord, help us hear each other with patience."* Modeling calm and spiritual leadership in the moment shows your spouse they are safe, even when emotions run high.

Chapter Two – Kindness: Choosing Gentle Words and Actions

Merriam-Webster defines kindness as "the quality of being friendly, generous, and considerate." In marriage, it's having a genuinely pleasant disposition toward, and being selfless and thoughtful with, your spouse. In Christian marriage, God is love, and a reliance on Him is what makes it possible to be the embodiment of the characteristics of kindness. A pleasant disposition, selflessness, and thoughtfulness are the obvious characteristics of kindness. The more obscure characteristics can look different than expected, such as a spouse's much-needed humor in the most trying of times.

Memories of childhood trauma sometimes made it difficult for kindness to be my first reaction as a spouse. My grandmother rarely spoke kindly to me, and the family friend who abused me was a wolf in sheep's clothing. I had trouble being kind growing up when a friend disagreed with me, and I carried resentment and distrust into my marriage. However, the more Marty and I allowed ourselves to be mentored by older Christian couples, the more we learned how to listen, truly listen, to the Father and to each other. God helped me by giving me something I never had in my home growing up, examples of kindness in marriage. This made me pause and rethink my words and actions.

My Aunt's Tribute to Kindness

Many people have the impression that God is only a fire and brimstone raining judge. He actually has many attributes, one of which is kindness, as He explained to Moses. "And the Lord passed by before him, and proclaimed, The Lord, The Lord God, merciful and gracious, longsuffering, and abundant in goodness and truth (Exodus 34:6 KJV)." Merriam-Webster defines graciousness as kindness. Still, my aunt had a very difficult time accepting the Lord as a kind God.

I was eight years old when my aunt joined the family. My uncle and I, who were raised by the same people, were seventeen years apart but very close. After a brief marriage to a lady who became lonely and sought love elsewhere while my uncle served in Vietnam, my uncle started dating again. He was attacked by a rabid cat and had to see the doctor for a series of shots. It was in the doctor's office that he met my aunt, a receptionist. He asked, "Would you like to join me for supper? I know a little French restaurant. It's called Jacques In Zee Box!" Intrigued by his humor, my aunt accepted his invitation. Somewhere in the course of their many conversations, my aunt shared the abuse of her childhood. My uncle, who never shed tears, cried that day. My aunt told me that was the moment she knew she was in love with him. They soon married and let me be the flower girl at their wedding.

Because of her past abuse, my aunt turned her back on God and claimed to be an atheist. One day after I said the blessing for my uncle and I before we ate a meal, my aunt looked at me and asked, "How can you pray to a God who lets such bad things happen to good people?"

"Leave her alone," my uncle scolded. "She has more faith in her pinky than you and I put together."

My uncle and I exchanged smiles, and my little heart knew he would be my hero for life. Still, I've never forgotten the pain I saw in my aunt's face, the pain that comes from being all too familiar with the bad that happens to good people.

I studied my aunt and uncle's relationship as I spent a great deal of time with them while I was growing up. Decades later, after my aunt's passing, people told me the thing they remembered most about her was her kindness. Five minutes after meeting her, they found themselves opening up and sharing their heart with her because of her kindness. In marriage, however, she struggled to show kindness to my uncle. Her past abuse, her resentment toward God, and the day-to-day hardships of life made it easy for her to lash out at my uncle. I guess a spouse can only take so much of that before he or she snaps, because that's what happened to my uncle. I was sixteen when I heard from my devastated aunt that my uncle had an affair with another woman. My aunt and uncle separated and moved hundreds of miles apart, each of them alone, for a year.

One day during a visit with my aunt, she asked me how I had been able to survive after everything I'd been through. I summed up my initial response in two words, my faith. I told her of people I'd read about that had such a profound impact on my young life, including Holocaust survivor Corrie ten Boom and disability activist Joni Eareckson Tada. I explained that in the face of overwhelming adversity, they stood on their faith in God and helped countless people do the same. My aunt agreed to meet with my uncle and my childhood pastor. They poured their hearts out in repentance to God and to each other, and renewed their wedding vows. God rewarded them with fifty years of a marriage built on learning kindness before their passing.

The Overwhelming Qualities of Boaz and Ruth

One would be hard pressed to find a greater couple's love story in the Bible than that of Boaz and Ruth (Ruth 1-4). Boaz is continually taken aback by Ruth's selflessness, as he indicates in Ruth 2:11b-12 "But I also know about everything you have done for your mother-in-law since the death of your husband. I have heard how you left your father and mother and your own land to live here among complete strangers. May the Lord, the God of Israel, under whose wings you have come to take refuge, reward you fully for what you have done."

Notice how Boaz uses gentle words to affirm Ruth's worth. He acknowledges God's sovereignty, and thus it is evident to him that Ruth takes refuge in God. Boaz demonstrates kindness to Ruth by making mention of her care for Naomi, by asking the Lord to bless her because of her kindness to Naomi, and by ensuring that Ruth will be protected. In marriage, kindness often looks like noticing the unseen sacrifices your spouse makes and affirming their value out loud.

Ruth shows gratitude instead of entitlement. She is overwhelmed by Boaz's genuine kindness in allowing her to gather grain behind his harvesters. As she and Boaz become close, Boaz confides in her that he knows she could have chosen a younger man to marry, but he's glad she chose him. Once married, they are blessed with a son who turns out to be the grandfather of King David, a forefather of Jesus.

The Overwhelming Qualities of You and Your Spouse

Keep the ability to see the best in each other and remember those qualities throughout your marriage. Marty has many talents, one of which is macrame. He painstakingly knotted a cord in a repeated pattern to make a giant wall clock for me before we were married. I was taken aback that anyone would selflessly go to such lengths to gift me with a token of his love. For years, the clock was a constant reminder, no matter how frustrated I got with Marty, that he was a good and caring man. In my frustration, I caught sight of the clock and was carried back to a time when I was left speechless by the extent of Marty's kindness. Even now, remembering the clock changes the way I respond when conflict arises by reminding me that Marty truly has a kind and caring heart. This demonstrates that kindness can greatly affect each other, both at the time the kindness is extended and long afterward when you hit bumps in the road. Hold onto these reminders of love.

Kindness doesn't always look like a soft word—it can also come through a well-timed laugh that eases tension and restores peace. Marty's gift of humor has been used throughout our marriage to bring kindness and comfort. When my family was shaken by sudden tragedy, his humor became a lifeline that carried us through.

Allow me to illustrate with a story. My grandfather remarried soon after my grandmother's passing. My step-grandmother succumbed to injuries sustained when she and my grandfather were hit head on by a drunk teenage driver. Our own kids were teenagers then. They flew out with Marty to San Diego for the memorial service.

I was already there. I hadn't slept or eaten in several days. Grief had worn me down, and I was fragile. In the middle of that haze, my aunt and I had a heated discussion over the phone. I didn't know anything about Lewy-Body dementia, or that she was suffering from the disease. All I knew was that she wasn't just a school psychologist. She was my confidant from my teenage years - now she felt like a stranger.

Tensions had been running high. She had recently clashed with a relative of my step-grandmother over something trivial, and as we began planning the memorial, I tried to keep the peace. My voice trembled as I said, "I don't want any fighting. Daddy (what I called my grandfather) doesn't need to be upset any more than he already is."

My aunt exploded. "You spoiled, selfish brat! Who do you think you are talking to me that way? After the accident, I took him into our home and cared for him, and this is the thanks I get? You should be ashamed of yourself."

Then she hung up. Just like that, the line went dead. I tried to call back, desperate to apologize for how I'd worded my plea, but she refused to answer. I couldn't eat. I couldn't sleep. I could only cry. A few days later when the family met to plan the memorial service, my aunt acted as though nothing had happened. "I don't know what's going on," my uncle whispered in my ear, "but I don't think she remembers that the two of you fought."

Exhausted and confused, I had Marty stay with my grandfather while I took the kids to church that Sunday. We would have normally gone to my childhood church, but a neighbor invited us to hers which was much closer, so we accepted the invitation. I failed to ask the neighbor what the attire was at her church. I took it for granted that we should wear our Sunday best. By the time I finally found where the church was located, we were the last to walk in. The only seats left were in the front row. As we sheepishly made our way down the aisle, we noticed that everyone but us was dressed in shorts and t-shirts. We cringed at the sight.

The praise team led the worship music that morning. They instructed us to turn in our songbooks to a specific page. The kids obliged and awkwardly started to giggle. The impetus was something they spied on the page, perhaps the name of the songwriter, but time has wiped it from my memory. "Be quiet," I leaned over and mumbled through clenched teeth.

My stern warning only made them giggle more. Tears flowed down their cheeks as they tried, to no avail, to stifle their laughter. I hung my head in embarrassment. Finally, one of the kids pointed to the item on the page that started their giggling, as if the sight would justify their rude behavior. Without missing a beat, I glanced at the item while still singing with the congregation. As the singing concluded and we were asked to take our seats for the sermon, guess who got the giggles? Mm-hmm. Yours Truly.

After service, in recognition of our appalling behavior, we tried to sneak out and never return. Our seats up front made that impossible. "What a delight it was to have such a jovial bunch in service with us this morning," the pastor said as he came and shook our hands. We were so stunned, we could barely respond.

"Well, we aim to please," I answered with a grimace. With that, we made our departure. (For the record, I visited that church again on one of my subsequent visits.)

Back at the house, I shared the church antics with Marty.

"The Lord knew how desperately you needed to laugh," he remarked.

The stress of the situation with my family, the church outing, and my aunt, was all building and building like a volcano about to erupt. I had a choice to erupt in anger or kindness. Sometimes kindness looks like laughter. Marty has taught me that. In the middle of the storms, his kindness calms me. The storms that are building up in and around me start to fade away. In marriage, couples need to be able to meet their mates where they are with that kindness.

It was too painful for me to watch my aunt deteriorate, both because of the relationship I lost and because of the inadvertent pain she caused me. Marty's internal joy and his way to bring the light to a hard situation was what I needed. "You may have to be the one to engage in conversations with my aunt from now on," I told him. "My heart aches to have my confidant again, but if her mind is going, you have that delicate cushion of humor she accepts."

Marty recognizes that when our hearts are weary with grief, strife, and confusion, God supplies the reprieve and comfort of joy. I admire that quality in him so much.

Many years later, just before our oldest grandkids were born, my grandfather passed away. At the cemetery, my aunt needed to sit down. She went to the van, and the rest of our family followed. The cemetery workers were in a rush, for some reason, to get my grandfather's body in the ground. They suspended the coffin in mid-air, positioned it over the hole in the ground, and lowered it all the way. However, they didn't get it lowered before my aunt mistakenly set off the car alarm. The horn blared and lights flashed, creating quite the spectacle. The more my aunt tried to correct her mistake, the more the alarm blared. My uncle rushed to the van and stopped the alarm. Right on cue and to ease my aunt's embarrassment, Marty said, "That's okay. We needed to send Bob out in style!"

Everyone, including my aunt, had a good laugh. That's why I so admire Marty's sense of humor. In the awkwardness of life, he unpacks the blanket of God's joy. Marty's light-hearted remark defused tension and gave the family a way to smile through tears. That was a gentle act of kindness in a moment of deep pain.

It's easy to proudly adjust the halo on your brow and become critical of your spouse when you're tired, generally irritable, and stressed, but resist the temptation. Take time to ask God to help you find the ways in which your spouse really is trying to support the marriage through kindness.

Because kindness is our focus here, it helps to see submission through that lens. Submission is not about power or control but about honoring one another with gentleness. Peter said to wives in 1 Peter 3:4-5, "You should clothe yourselves instead with the beauty that comes from within, the unfading beauty of a gentle and quiet spirit, which is so precious to God. This is how the holy women of old made themselves beautiful. They put their trust in God and accepted the authority of their husbands."

Before you roll your eyes, ladies, nothing takes my husband's breath away like my submission by choosing kindness over harshness. Gentleness is kindness lived out. Instead of sharp words or a demanding spirit, submission shows kindness by choosing peace and building up rather than tearing down. Though it takes much more strength to keep my mouth shut than to fly off the handle, I've learned that kindness often speaks more powerfully than sharp words. If I had discovered sooner that gentle kindness could shape the atmosphere of our home and childrearing, it would have saved us many unnecessary wounds. Proverbs 31:26: "She opens her mouth with wisdom, and the teaching of kindness is on her tongue."

As I mentioned before, Marty is the chief cook in our home. He collects gadgets for the kitchen. I am the chief dishwasher. I clean the gadgets he brings home. I find it easier to place the gadgets in a pile for him to put away than to find places for them myself. That gets on his one last nerve. The old me would have shrieked, "I don't care how much it gets on your nerves! I didn't bring the gadgets home. I probably won't ever use them. Isn't it enough that I wash them? Why should I be the one to put them away? What do you think I am, a doormat that you can just wipe your feet on whenever you wish?" Kindness doesn't always come naturally. It often requires a pause, a prayer, and a willingness to put your spouse's feelings before your own.

Today, before I allow myself to get too far in sounding like the old me, the new me asks God for strength to be quiet, surrender to God's heart and choose kindness over conflict. I simply find homes for the gadgets. Marty walks into a clean kitchen, gasps with a smile, and takes me out to eat!

Mutual kindness balances the relationship. To husbands, 1 Peter 3:7 says, "In the same way, you husbands must give honor to your wives. Treat your wife with kindness and understanding as you live together. She is your equal partner in God's gift of new life. Treat her as you should so your prayers will not be hindered." In our home, kindness looks as simple as me putting away kitchen gadgets that get on my nerves, and Marty honoring me with chivalry and tenderness. That is the power of choosing kindness over conflict.

Summary

Kindness in marriage may not always be our first instinct—especially when past wounds or childhood trauma have shaped us to react with defensiveness, sharp words, or resentment. Yet God, in His grace, teaches us to pause, lean into His Spirit, and let our words and actions reflect His gentleness instead of our pain.

The story of Boaz and Ruth reminds us that kindness often looks like noticing unseen sacrifices and speaking life over one another. Their love story shows us the power of affirming words, gratitude instead of entitlement, and compassion that protects and provides. In marriage, these same qualities bring strength and security.

Through humor in times of grief, chivalry in moments of fear, or quiet submission that chooses peace over strife, kindness becomes a cycle that blesses both husband and wife. It softens hard seasons, carries us through loss, and reminds us that we are not alone.

Kindness in marriage is strength clothed in gentleness. It is a choice, again and again, to build up rather than tear down. When we allow God's kindness to shape our words and actions, we not only honor our spouse but also honor Christ, who modeled for us the greatest act of selfless love.

Chapter 2 Questions:

Reflect on the questions below about how kindness plays a part in your marriage. Use the space provided to capture your thoughts. Discuss them with your spouse if you both agree.

Boaz noticed Ruth's unseen sacrifices and spoke blessings over her. What unseen sacrifices has your spouse made recently, and how might you affirm them out loud?

Ruth responded with gratitude instead of entitlement. How can you guard your own heart against entitlement and nurture thankfulness in your marriage?

When you remember a past act of kindness from your spouse—like Marty's handmade clock—how does it soften your frustration during moments of conflict?

What "reminders of love" do you have in your home or heart that point you back to your spouse's character and care?

How can small, thoughtful gestures (like a handmade gift or act of service) continue to nurture long-term kindness between you and your spouse?

How has humor helped to ease tension or bring comfort in your own marriage?

How might laughter be one of God's gifts of kindness during difficult seasons?

How does your treatment of your spouse—whether through kindness, respect, or humility—shape your spiritual life and your prayers?

This week, how can you, like Boaz and Ruth, choose to "see the best" in your spouse and respond with kindness that will echo into the future of your marriage?

When stress builds like a storm inside you, how do your words change—and what might kindness look like in those moments?

In what ways has your spouse shown quiet patience when you were wounded, weary, or difficult to love?

Where does your past still try to teach you to protect yourself instead of trusting your spouse?

How do your reactions in conflict reflect what's happening inside your heart more than what's happening in your marriage?

When you feel most misunderstood, do you lean toward withdrawal or harshness—and what would gentleness require instead?

How does choosing kindness challenge your pride more than "winning" ever could?

Where have you been tempted to adjust your halo outwardly while your heart resists inward change?

How does your tone shift when you feel powerless—and how could kindness restore your sense of peace?

In times when laughter seems inappropriate, how might God actually be offering it as healing?

What is one area of conflict where kindness has the power to change the atmosphere more than logic ever could?

How do you tend to respond when your spouse disappoints you—and what might grace look like instead?

What does your spouse need from you emotionally right now that you may not have acknowledged?

When you choose gentle silence instead of sharp words, how does it affect your spirit later?

How does kindness toward your spouse shape the emotional climate of your home?

If your halo reflects the way you love, what would your spouse say it reveals about Christ in you?

Trauma Awareness: Kindness

For someone who has lived through trauma, kindness is not just a pleasant extra — it is essential for safety. A trauma survivor's nervous system is often on high alert. What may sound like a harmless joke, sarcasm, or a sharp tone to one person can register as a threat to the survivor, even if the one delivering the message doesn't mean it that way. This is because past abuse or neglect trained their body to brace for attack. Even when no danger is present, the nervous system reacts as though there is.

Kindness, on the other hand, helps calm the survivor's body and mind. Gentle tones, affirming words, and thoughtful gestures signal safety. Humor can be an especially powerful form of kindness when it is lighthearted. A shared laugh tells the survivor: "You're safe with me. We can enjoy this moment together."

Small acts of kindness also build trust. When a spouse makes the bed, prepares a cup of coffee, or puts away kitchen gadgets without complaint, these simple gestures communicate consistency and care. For a survivor, those actions re-train the heart to believe: "This person sees me, values me, and won't abandon me."

Scripture reminds us, "Gracious words are a honeycomb, sweet to the soul and healing to the bones" (Proverbs 16:24). In the same way, small acts of humor and kindness bring sweetness and healing — often in places where old wounds once whispered fear.

Tool: Soft Start-Ups

The purpose of soft start-ups is to help couples begin sensitive conversations in ways that feel safe rather than threatening.

Steps:

1. **Pause First.** Before you speak, take a breath and ask yourself: *Am I about to criticize, or can I affirm first?*

2. **Lead With Kindness.** Start the conversation by expressing appreciation or admiration.
    - Example: *"I love the way you care about our family."*

3. **State the Concern Gently.** Use "I" statements rather than "you" statements.
    - Example: *"I feel overwhelmed when the bills pile up. Could we sit down and plan together?"*

4. **Invite Dialogue.** End with an open question that allows your spouse to share their perspective.
    - Example: *"What do you think would help us handle this better?"*

"A gentle answer turns away wrath, but a harsh word stirs up anger." Proverbs 15:1

Journal about one trigger you identified. What memory or feeling might be beneath it? Invite God to bring healing there.

Exercise: The Daily Kindness Challenge

As couples, we must train ourselves to show consistent, small acts of kindness to build trust, safety, and connection with each other.

Steps:
1. Choose Your Kindness. Each day, decide on two acts:
    a. One Verbal Affirmation. Speak one specific encouragement (e.g., "You always make me laugh when I need it most.").
    b. One Small Act of Service. Do something tangible (e.g., bring a snack, handle a chore, leave a kind note).

Look for opportunities to share gentle moments — or even laughter to create emotional safety and ease tension.

2. Notice the Impact. Pay attention to your spouse's response. Did they relax, smile, or soften? These are signs their nervous system felt safe.

3. Reflect Together. At the end of the week, share with each other which affirmations, acts of service, or lighthearted moments meant the most.

Repeat Daily. Continue until kindness becomes a natural rhythm of your marriage.

"Dear children, let us not love with words or speech but with actions and in truth" (1 John 3:18). The Daily Kindness Challenge puts this verse into practice by combining one affirmation with one tangible act of service each day.

At the end of the week, ask: When did pausing help us avoid an argument? How did praying together change the tone of our discussion?

Trauma Support Application

As the supporting spouse, your role is to make kindness both **felt and consistent**. For someone with a trauma history, your tone, timing, and small daily actions matter as much as your words. Sarcasm, harshness, or neglect of follow-through can easily be misread by their nervous system as threat or abandonment. Your steady kindness retrains their body to believe, *"I am safe, I am seen, I am valued."*

- **Start gently.** Begin sensitive conversations with affirmation before addressing concerns. A soft tone and a relaxed posture help your spouse's body feel safe to listen. If your words come out sharp, pause and repair: "That came out wrong, let me try again."

- **Layer kindness into daily rhythms.** Commit to one affirmation and one small act of service every day. Predictability is powerful—it communicates, *"I'll show up for you again tomorrow."*

- **Use humor carefully.** Shared laughter can melt tension, but only when it feels light and safe. Aim for humor that includes rather than embarrasses, and always check your spouse's response before continuing.

- **Notice body cues.** A softened face, a sigh, or a small smile signals that your kindness is landing. A tightened jaw or clipped answers mean it's time to slow down, reassure, or simply offer presence instead of words.

- **Close the loop.** At the end of each week, ask: "Which words or gestures made you feel most cared for? How can I keep building on that?" This not only strengthens connection, but also reassures your spouse that kindness will continue.

Kindness in your role doesn't always mean big displays or showy niceties. Most times, it's about steady presence, consistent gentleness, and being intentional with your words and actions until safety becomes the natural atmosphere of your marriage.

Chapter Three – Contentment: Guarding against Envy

Envy, in general, is that uneasy, resentful feeling that arises when we see someone else having or enjoying something we want for ourselves. It's not just wishing we had what they have — that's desire. Envy goes further: it carries comparison, discontent, and even bitterness toward the person who has what we lack. Envy in marriage is more than wishing you had what your spouse has — most of the time you are sharing things with your spouse. It's really the resentment that creeps in when you compare yourself to your spouse instead of celebrating them. Scripture puts it simply: "Love does not envy" (1 Corinthians 13:4). In the mind's eye of the spouse who feels resentful or envious, a sarcastic halo appears on the other spouse's brow.

Envy can look like feelings of irritation when your spouse is praised or successful, comparing your own background, talents, or achievements against theirs or even resenting the attention, opportunities, or personality strengths your spouse has. Envy shifts your focus from unity to competition. It creates distance instead of connection, and it blinds you to the blessings God has given your marriage. For trauma survivors especially, envy can also stem from unhealed wounds — for example, envying a spouse's stable childhood or calmness because those things feel out of reach.

Guarding Against Envy

Guarding against envy means intentionally replacing comparison with gratitude and admiration. Instead of seeing your spouse's strengths as a threat, view them as part of the gift God gave you when He joined you together as one. The truth is that you and your spouse are not competitors — you are one flesh. That means their growth is your growth, and their blessing is your blessing. One of the best ways to guard against envy is to become your spouse's spiritual encourager. When you fight for their faith; praying with them, cheering for their spiritual victories, and standing firm during their struggles, you stop competing and start celebrating. Fighting for their faith turns comparison into partnership.

I was only 34 when I had a total hysterectomy. Once I was home from the hospital, Marty knelt down beside my recliner, took my hand, and looked into my eyes with such love as he spoke. "I know you might feel like less of a woman, but there's no way you could be less of a woman to me." As I brushed away tears, he showered me with plenty of reading material from our local Christian bookstore. He graciously fed my self-esteem, but even more importantly, he remembered to feed my faith.

Along with the emotional toll of my surgery, I had some questions for God as well. Why was He allowing the hysterectomy while Marty and I were in our prime? Why was Marty getting to keep his virility while, in my mind, I was being put out to pasture? Because of my eight years of childhood sexual abuse, it took me forever to become even remotely comfortable being intimate. Why was that already being taken away? The reading material from Marty brought me peace and pointed me to the answers.

The hysterectomy was all a splendid part of God's plan. I had to lean on God to fill the void left by my surgery, and as a result, my Lord and I grew closer. Marty and I together grew closer to God and to each other as we navigated uncharted waters. Most importantly, we were able to minister to other questioning couples because of our experience.

In sharp contrast, Job's wife allows herself to become an instrument of the enemy toward her husband. In Job 2:9, she says, "Are you still trying to maintain your integrity? Curse God and die."

Can't you just see a halo on her brow, as though she, not Job, was the expert on how to handle the loss? Job loses everything that he owns, he loses his children, and he is suffering with boils all over his body. The last thing he needs is for his wife to make the statement she makes. Before we come down too hard on her, though, remember that she suffers the same loss as Job, with the exception of her health. When we're in the throes of grief, isn't it easy to let the pain do the talking? Imagine the difference in the story if Job's wife responds like Hannah. In her anguish, Hannah completely pours out her heart to the Lord, and is rewarded for her faith (1 Samuel 1:15-17). Imagine the morale booster for Job if his wife had said, "I know we're suffering great loss, but God has never failed to be there for us, and He won't fail us now." That's why we need to fight for our spouse's faith.

The Reward

When Marty graduated from college, I quit my job at the Library for the Blind and Handicapped so we could move to where there were more job opportunities for Marty. While waiting to hear from principals who had interviewed him for teaching positions, Marty took a grocery store job. Sadly, he came down with pleurisy and had to quit. We then learned I was expecting our first child. As Marty was writhing in anguish in bed with pleurisy, I was in bed beside him with horrible morning sickness, and we didn't know how we would make ends meet, Marty said, "I don't understand. We've been begging and pleading for God to intervene on our behalf, and He hasn't."

"Paul and Silas sang praises from their jail cell," I reminded Marty (Acts 16:25). "God graciously freed them. Let's start praising."

We held hands and wept our adoration to the Lord. Suddenly, the phone rang. Marty answered it and looked at me in astonishment. It was a principal offering Marty a teaching position! Not only that, but Marty's pleurisy and my morning sickness disappeared. We were over the moon at the way God honored our obedience. I believe God gave me the words to encourage Marty's faith and not allow succumbing to despair. Fighting for your spouse's faith is so worthwhile.

Summary

Instead of becoming an instrument of the enemy toward your spouse, fight for your spouse's faith. The enemy delights in sowing division through comparison, criticism, or resentment, but you have the power to guard against envy by standing shoulder to shoulder in prayer. In moments of anguish, pour your heart out completely to the Lord — not only for your needs, but for the strengthening of your spouse's spirit.

When you encourage your spouse's faith, you disarm envy at its root. Their blessings no longer feel like losses to you; they become victories for your marriage. Their growth no longer threatens you; it inspires you. Feeding your spouse's faith is an act of kindness, humility, and unity — it reminds both of you that you are not opponents, but partners in God's calling.

As you fight for each other's faith, you will see how God blesses you both — not only with spiritual growth, but with deeper intimacy, greater contentment, and joy in celebrating each other's strengths as gifts from His hand. Remember the truth of Ecclesiastes 4:9–10: *"Two are better than one, because they have a good return for their labor: If either of them falls down, one can help the other up."*

Chapter 3 Questions:

Reflect on the questions below about how you think envy can impact your marriage. Use the space provided to capture your thoughts. Discuss them with your spouse if you both agree.

When your spouse succeeds, receives praise, or shines in an area where you struggle, what is your first emotional reaction — joy, pride, or something else like irritation or insecurity?

How might unhealed wounds from your past feed feelings of envy toward your spouse's strengths or blessings (for example, envying their calmness, stable upbringing, or spiritual maturity)?

What are some subtle ways envy might show up in your words or actions — perhaps in sarcasm, withholding praise, or trying to "one-up" your spouse?

How would your marriage look different if you saw your spouse's strengths as part of the gift God gave you when He made you one flesh?

In what ways does envy shift your mindset from unity to competition, and how has that affected your emotional closeness?

How does the truth that "Love does not envy" (1 Corinthians 13:4) challenge your current perspective on your spouse's talents and achievements?

Reflect on the story of Job and his wife. How might her response have changed the atmosphere in their suffering if she had spoken words of faith instead of despair?

Think about a time your spouse was discouraged. Did you respond more like Job's wife or like Hannah, who poured her anguish out to God in 1 Samuel 1?

How could you become a spiritual encourager to your spouse—what specific actions (praying together, sharing Scripture, speaking affirmations) could you start this week?

What are three specific strengths or blessings in your spouse that you can thank God for today instead of comparing yourself to them?

How might expressing admiration out loud (rather than silently feeling inferior) disarm envy in your heart and build unity in your marriage? How could celebrating your spouse's growth as "your shared victory" change the emotional tone in your relationship?

Trauma Awareness: Contentment

For trauma survivors, envy often grows from wounds left by the past. It is not simply wanting what someone else has; it is the ache of feeling "less than." Survivors may envy a spouse's calmness, emotional stability, family background, or even their faith journey — because these things feel out of reach.

The nervous system, shaped by neglect or abuse, is quick to interpret differences as threats. Instead of celebrating a spouse's strength, the survivor may feel exposed in their weakness. This creates an internal narrative of: "They have what I don't — and I will never measure up." There can even be a body-level reaction to feeling "not enough." When a spouse's strengths highlight a survivor's insecurities, the nervous system may interpret it as threat rather than blessing. Their brain remembers: "I wasn't safe then… I'm probably not safe now." Gratitude interrupts that cycle. It is a grounding tool that brings the nervous system back to connection.

Envy, left unchecked, can deepen shame and isolation. But when couples guard against envy, they learn to turn comparison into admiration and gratitude. Fighting for each other's faith is one of the most powerful antidotes: it transforms envy into encouragement, reminding both spouses they are one flesh, not competitors. Scripture says plainly: "Love does not envy" (1 Corinthians 13:4). Guarding against envy is really guarding the unity of your marriage.

Tool: Reframe the Difference

Gratitude and envy cannot coexist in your nervous system. Gratitude signals safety; envy signals threat. You choose which one leads your heart. Turn envy-triggering comparisons into opportunities for gratitude and growth.

Steps:

1. **Notice the Envy**—When you feel irritation, comparison, or resentment toward your spouse, pause and name it: "I'm feeling envy right now."
2. **Identify the Trigger**—Ask yourself: "What about my spouse is stirring this feeling? Is it their calmness, background, success, attention, or strength?"
3. **Reframe**—Shift the narrative: Instead of "I lack what they have," reframe it as "This is a gift God has given my spouse that blesses our marriage."
4. **Replace with Admiration**—Speak out one sentence of gratitude or admiration toward your spouse for that very quality.
   Example: "Your calmness steadies me when I feel anxious. I'm grateful God gave you that gift."

Exercise: The Blessing List

Be proactive to identify a quick go-to list to fight envy with gratitude and celebration.

Steps:

1. **List Traits Weekly**—Once a week, each spouse writes down three qualities, strengths, or gifts they see in the other.
2. **Share Aloud**—Read the lists to one another. Allow space for encouragement and affirmation.
3. **Pray Over Each Other**—Thank God for the traits on your spouse's list, and ask Him to deepen and multiply those gifts in their life.
4. **Reflect Together**—Discuss how those strengths make your marriage stronger — so their blessing becomes your blessing.

Optional reflection step: For couples where envy is rooted in deep trauma wounds (e.g., envying a spouse's safe childhood), include a gentle conversation prompt like:

> "When I see the stability you had growing up, I feel the ache of what I missed. But I'm learning to thank God that you can now provide that stability in our marriage and family."

"For where you have envy and selfish ambition, there you find disorder and every evil practice." (James 3:16)

Envy doesn't just make us feel unsettled — it invites disorder into our marriage. It blinds us to blessings, stirs up competition, and creates distance instead of unity. Guarding against envy means inviting God's wisdom into your relationship, where peace, humility, and contentment take the place of comparison.

Verse 17 of that passage reads, "But the wisdom that comes from heaven is first of all pure; then peace-loving, considerate, submissive, full of mercy and good fruit, impartial and sincere."

When you fight for your spouse's faith — encouraging their growth, celebrating their strengths, and standing with them in prayer — you are pushing back against the disorder envy brings. In its place, you cultivate peace, gratitude, and deeper intimacy.

Trauma Support Application

For a trauma survivor, envy isn't always about material possessions or accomplishments. Sometimes it is about longing for the stability, calmness, or sense of belonging they never had growing up. Watching a spouse move through life with ease, or enjoy healthy family ties, can stir feelings of inadequacy or resentment—even if they deeply love and admire you. Your role as the supportive spouse is to help shift the atmosphere from comparison to gratitude, creating space where your partner feels secure instead of "less than."

- **Affirm their value.** When you notice your spouse comparing themselves to you or others, gently redirect with specific affirmations: *"You bring a perspective and strength I never would have on my own."*

- **Reframe differences as gifts.** Speak aloud how your differences make the marriage stronger, rather than threatening. Example: *"Your cautiousness balances my impulsiveness—we're better together."*

- **Model gratitude out loud.** Make thankfulness visible. Share what you appreciate about your spouse in front of others, and especially in private, so they can internalize it as truth.

- **Avoid dismissive comparisons.** Never say, *"You shouldn't feel that way,"* or *"At least you have…"* These statements reinforce shame. Instead, validate and then reframe: *"I understand why that stings. I also see the unique ways God is using you."*

- **Ground in Scripture together.** Remind your spouse that God designed both of you with intention. "I praise you because I am fearfully and wonderfully made" (Psalm 139:14) applies to your spouse's story as much as anyone's. Read it aloud together in moments of envy or insecurity.

- **Celebrate small wins.** Survivors may overlook their own progress. Point it out—whether it's handling a stressful situation with more calm, or choosing gratitude in a tough moment. These reminders anchor hope.

When you practice contentment as the supportive spouse, you are not just easing envy—you are helping your partner rewrite the story trauma once told them: *"I am lacking."* Your steady encouragement helps them believe instead: *"I am enough, and together, we are blessed."*

Chapter Four – Humility: Letting Go of the Need to Impress

Humility is not thinking less of yourself — it's thinking of yourself less. In marriage, humility means choosing to value your spouse's heart above your own pride. It's resisting the urge to "win" an argument, to prove you're right, or to demand recognition. Instead, humility focuses on serving, listening, and building up your spouse.

Scripture says, "Do nothing out of selfish ambition or vain conceit. Rather, in humility value others above yourselves" (Philippians 2:3). This principle is the foundation of unity in marriage. When you lay down the need to impress or dominate, you make room for tenderness, respect, and deeper intimacy. In Matthew 11:29, Jesus says, "Take my yoke upon you. Let me teach you, because I am humble and gentle at heart, and you will find rest for your souls." Because He is the epitome of humility, we can emulate His example of service and putting another's needs above our own.

Humility in marriage is not a weakness; it's strength under control. It's the courage to admit fault, the wisdom to let go of the need to be right, and the love to prioritize your spouse's feelings over your own ego.

The Rift

Humility sounds simple in theory, but it is tested in the everyday moments where pride pushes us to prove a point. The need to be right, to be seen as competent, or to hold the upper hand in an argument can quietly take priority over the heart of our spouse. That's where humility is either lived out—or lost.

In our marriage, this lesson came at a steep cost. Pride had us both locked in a battle of words, each trying to justify ourselves instead of cherishing each other. The result was not just a messy house; it was a rift between our spirits. Our misplaced priorities nearly tore us apart until God reminded us that humility means letting go of the need to impress and choosing instead to guard one another's hearts.

"I can be here with the kids an entire day and keep the house immaculate." With that, I was nearly blinded by the tilted halo resting on Marty's brow as he made this remark on numerous occasions when coming home. However, it was true. Once our kids were born, housework did not get top priority in my book, not even close. I was wholly consumed with working-mom guilt, though by then, society had become much more accepting of mothers who worked outside the home. I preferred spending time doing things the kids and I enjoyed over cleaning the house. This became a source of contention in our marriage, so much so that we attacked each other verbally.

Marty would say something like, "You can't be so stupid that you can't see that this house is a pigsty!"

I would boldly answer, "You can't be so stupid that you can't see that the kids aren't getting to know you!"

We soon hired a periodic house cleaner, but the problem went deeper than a dirty home. We had crushed each other's spirit. For me, Marty's words were a blow to my self-esteem, and the hurt of being accused of doing a terrible job with my wifely duties. My grandmother's ranting from childhood that I would grow up to be as hopeless as my birth mother reverberated in my mind's ear. For Marty, he felt disrespected, and the hurt of being accused of doing a terrible job as a father. The awareness of how damaging our words were didn't come right away. We each needed to have time to think and pray. Once we surrendered our pride to God, we were able to listen and speak to each other with thoughtfulness. What helped us learn to forgive harsh words and not hold onto them were the first three chapters of Romans. They explain that because people historically were so insistent on things like quarreling, God gave them over to their foolish ways. We quarrel as carelessly as if typing a document, and in haste upon completion, inadvertently clicking Don't Save instead of Save. The document is lost. Likewise, we lose our ability to think of others and, according to Romans, we exhibit behaviors or sins (like quarreling) that prove that we're living only for ourselves. The reward for sin is death (Romans 3:23), but the reward for obedience to God is eternal life through Jesus.

It was true that I never did much to help our kids learn to do dishes. When I was fourteen and my grandmother had her fatal heart attack, we were arguing over the dishes I'd left undone. I decided then that dirty dishes weren't worth having a heart attack over, and I carried that line of thinking into childrearing. As far as I was concerned, that was a sacred cow Marty just had to learn to let go.

As a couple, Marty and I had to take a time-out. We sought God's healing and realized the following: Married people are beings with feelings, and when you insist on being justified in behaving in a hurtful manner at the expense of your spouse's feelings, you bring a rift to your relationship. Rather, a heart that is fully surrendered to God is acutely sensitive to this, acknowledging His readiness to forgive, and is persuaded to be Johnny-on-the-spot to forgive the spouse. Don't let your need to be right (pride) be greater than your spouse's feelings. Only you and God may know the intentions of your heart, and that's enough. Marty learned to overlook some clutter. I learned to do my work while the kids slept, and our family survived. When the kids were growing up, I explained the backstory of my grandmother's death to Marty. He came to understand the extent to which that experience influenced my perspective on chores. If you are a couple arguing over housework (for example) and you're not sure if there's a deeper wound beneath it, make it a matter of prayer.

This applies not only to marriage, but to relationships in general. In the story of Sarah and Hagar (Genesis 16), Sarah treats Hagar so harshly that Hagar runs away. This is the result of Sarah's inability to trust God's timing in making Abraham the father of many nations. Her inability to have children, combined with her advanced age, causes her to use Hagar as a surrogate for Abraham's child instead of waiting on God to give them one. It is while Hagar is taunting her barren boss that Sarah snaps. She treats Hagar so harshly that Hagar runs away. While on the run, she encounters an angel who tells her that God sees her. He doesn't want her to run away, but to return, submit to Sarah, and give birth to a son, Ishmael, who will also have many descendants because he is Abraham's child. Hagar complies. The takeaway from this story is that God is Jehovah El Roi (the God Who Sees Me). He knows what you've been through. He can shed light on the correlation of past trauma to present frustration. This is not to say to lose your playfulness, but there's a difference between being playful and maliciously poking fun at each other. It isn't God's desire that we maliciously taunt each other or treat each other harshly, but that we stop living for ourselves.

Misplaced Priorities

This was probably one of the hardest lessons for me to learn in the early days of our marriage. My constant need to prove my competency interfered with every Christian principle that was the foundation of our relationship. Marty and I came to blows over the silliest things because I had misplaced priorities. Once I finally learned that my "rightness" wasn't more important than Marty's feelings, it was almost too late. While divorce wasn't what either of us wanted, we almost couldn't find a way around it. Being right isn't more important than a person's heart, or than a lifetime commitment.

Recently, I needed clarification on how to handle an urgent financial matter. When I asked Marty about it, he was very short with me. He then grabbed his things and left in a huff for his part-time job. The old me would have been so hurt that I would have stewed over Marty's behavior all day, until I worked myself into a tirade to justify my rightness. Instead of succumbing to my old habits, I focused on what was most important, grace. I immediately asked God to help me forgive Marty. A while later, I heard my cell phone notifying me of a text message. Humility allows for grace, forgiveness and love to settle arguments, heal wounds and make space for you to grow together with God.

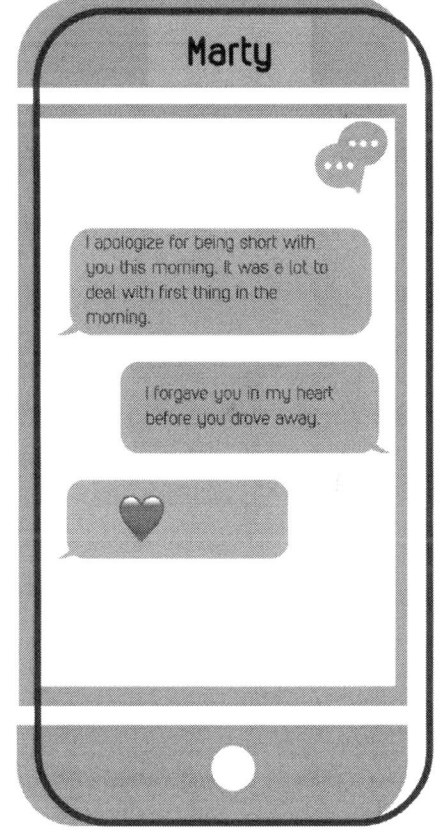

Vitamins and Cradles

What does the Bible have to say about this? Proverbs 31:11 says, "Her husband can trust her, and she will greatly enrich his life." Colossians 3:19 says, "Husbands, love your wives and never treat them harshly." According to these verses, no matter how right you think you are, God wants you to lay that aside.

Women, be like vitamins on steroids for your husband. When you walk into your phone carrier's store and ask for an upgrade, they don't bring you an antique model. Instead, they bring you the more modern versions of your phone. What can you do to refresh your husband?

Men, cradle the fragile shell of your wife's feelings. A bird will provide as many layers as it takes to keep its egg from getting broken. No matter how angry you get with your wife, do everything you can to keep the shell of her feelings intact. She may seem like granite, but she is really fine China.

Mary and Joseph

Matthew 1:18-24 describes Mary, the mother of Jesus, as a virgin engaged to a righteous man named Joseph. By the Holy Spirit, Mary becomes pregnant before she and Joseph are married. To spare Mary public disgrace, though he loves her dearly, Joseph makes the difficult decision to quietly break the engagement. However, before he can, he has an encounter with an angel in a dream. The angel reveals that because the baby was miraculously conceived by the Holy Spirit, Joseph should not be afraid to wed. Mary will give birth to a son, Jesus, who will save people from their sins. The angel also visits Mary and reveals the same splendid message to her (Luke 1). Joseph follows the angel's instructions, ushering the Messiah into the world.

Joseph could have shamed Mary for being unmarried and pregnant. Instead, he practices humility and accepts God's plan. Despite the risk of being ostracized in her community, Mary embraces her role. Both she and Joseph put aside their reputation and comfort for God's plan, thereby modeling humility. They trust God and support each other.

Summary

Humility in marriage means valuing your spouse's heart above your own pride. C.S. Lewis described humility best with the notion that it's not thinking less of *yourself* but thinking of yourself *less*; choosing to listen, serve, and build up rather than to win arguments or prove your worth. Pride seeks to be right; humility seeks to protect the relationship.

The lack of humility creates rifts: words become weapons, and proving competence can overshadow love. In my marriage, conflicts over housework revealed deeper issues of pride, misplaced priorities, and old wounds (like the trauma surrounding my grandmother's death). Only when Marty and I sought God's healing and forgiveness did I learn to release the need to be right and focus on guarding each other's hearts.

Humility is strength under control. It admits fault, forgives quickly, and prioritizes unity over ego. Scripture calls both spouses to practice this: wives enriching their husbands' lives like "vitamins," and husbands protecting their wives' hearts like "fragile shells." The example of Mary and Joseph shows humility in action: they set aside their personal reputation to trust God's plan and support each other.

Ultimately, humility creates the space for tenderness, respect, and deeper intimacy. Pride builds walls; humility builds connection. Work hard to keep from letting your need to be right become greater than your spouse's feelings. Both you and your spouse can find ways to help the marriage run more smoothly. Acknowledge God's readiness to forgive you, stay focused on what is most important (grace), and be ready to forgive your spouse. Husbands, don't be harsh with your wife, and wives, give your husband's life an upgrade.

Chapter 4 Questions:

Reflect on the questions below about how humility has shown itself in your marriage. Use the space provided to capture your thoughts. Discuss them with your spouse if you both agree.

When a disagreement arises, do you feel a stronger drive to be understood or to understand your spouse? What does that reveal about your heart?

How often do you equate being "right" with being "worthy"? How might that belief be harming your connection?

In what situations do you most struggle to let go of your need to "win"? Why do you think that is?

Can you recall a time when your words were technically correct, but emotionally wounding? What did that moment cost your relationship?

How have your past experiences (like childhood trauma or old family patterns) shaped how you respond when you feel criticized or disrespected?

Do you see places where your pride might be masking fear—fear of being seen as weak, incompetent, or not enough?

What might it look like, in a current area of conflict, to lay down your need to be right in order to protect your spouse's heart?

How would your tone or body language change if your goal was to build up your spouse rather than defend yourself?

When was the last time you sincerely admitted fault to your spouse? What was their response? How did it affect your closeness?

Do you tend to value tasks, appearances, or being competent more than the emotional well-being of your spouse? How could that be reversed?

If you set aside the need to impress your spouse (or others), what would change about the way you love and serve them?

What is one "sacred cow" in your home or habits that you might need to surrender for the sake of unity and peace?

How quickly do you forgive your spouse compared to how quickly you want to be forgiven?

How does knowing that God sees and understands your heart free you from needing your spouse to recognize your "rightness"?

Like Mary and Joseph, what would it look like for you to lay down your pride and reputation to support God's plan for your marriage?

Trauma Awareness: Humility

Pride and the need to be "right" often develop in trauma survivors as protective strategies. If you grew up in an environment where your voice was silenced or your worth was questioned, proving yourself becomes a way to guard against shame. But in marriage, this survival strategy can crush intimacy. Constantly trying to win arguments or prove competence makes your spouse feel small, unloved, or unworthy.

Humility is not about weakness or being a doormat. It is about laying down the armor of self-protection and trusting that your spouse — and ultimately God — can hold space for your vulnerabilities. Humility in a trauma-affected marriage looks like choosing your spouse's heart over your ego, listening without correcting, and choosing connection over competition.

Tool: Three Questions Before Responding

It is a conditioned response to react quickly because a trauma survivor learned long ago that hesitation wasn't safe. When conflict arises, the brain shifts into protection mode, and the survivor may respond defensively, impulsively, or with heightened emotion before they even realize what's happening.

It is important for both of you to take a deep breath in tense times to reset your minds and your bodies before continuing the discussion.

Steps:

1. **Ask Yourself Three Questions:**
   - *Have I listened fully to my spouse?*
   - *Am I about to respond to their pain or just defend my pride?*
   - *Is this the right moment, or do I need time to process first?*
2. **Choose a Humble Response.** If needed, say: *"I hear you, and I need a moment to think about this before I respond."* This prevents impulsive words that damage connection.

3. **Circle Back.** When calm, return to the conversation with gentleness, focusing on understanding your spouse rather than proving yourself.

Exercise: Humility in Action Challenge

Many couples could use a refresher in demonstrating humility in the marriage. The key is to practice putting your spouse's heart above your need to be right before it is the topic of an argument. Then it becomes a natural response.

Steps:

1. **Think back and identify a tough moment you have had with your spouse.** Maybe it is a recurring disagreement or an area where you usually feel the urge to prove yourself (housework, finances, parenting).
2. **Shift the Goal.** As you replay this incident, instead of aiming to "win," aim to understand your spouse's feelings in that moment. Put yourself in their place.
3. **Offer a Humble Act.** Think of one small action that communicates: *"Your feelings matter more than my pride."* Put this in practice when you feel that need arise to be right or win the argument.
   - Example: Listening without interrupting, doing a chore without being asked, or offering an apology before being asked for one.
4. **Reflect Together.** At the end of the week, talk with your spouse about how those acts of humility impacted your connection.
5. **Pray Together.** Ask God to help you keep laying down the need to impress and to build your marriage on humility and grace.

Ephesians 4:2 calls us *to "Be completely humble and gentle; be patient, bearing with one another in love."* This verse captures the very heart of humility in marriage. Humility is not about weakness or being walked on: it's about choosing gentleness over harsh words, patience over irritation, and love over the need to prove yourself right. When we lay down pride and release the pressure to perform or impress, we create space for grace. In that space, our spouse feels seen, valued, and safe.

<u>Trauma Support Application</u>

For survivors, humility in marriage can feel complicated. Past experiences of being silenced, dismissed, or ridiculed may make them wary of "lowering their guard." They may confuse humility with weakness, or fear that admitting fault will invite criticism or rejection. As the supportive spouse, your role is to make humility safe—by showing that vulnerability will be met with compassion, not attack.

- **Listen without correction.** When your spouse shares their story or perspective, resist the urge to "set the record straight." Humility means valuing their feelings over your need to defend. Respond with *"I hear you"* or *"That makes sense you'd feel that way."*
- **Validate before offering perspective.** Survivors often expect their experiences to be minimized. Break that pattern by affirming first: *"I can see how painful that must have been."* Only after validation should you gently share your own view, if needed.
- **Model admission of faults.** Go first in acknowledging mistakes. When you say, *"I was wrong there, and I'm sorry,"* you create an atmosphere where humility feels safe instead of shameful.
- **Avoid shaming language.** Words like *"overreacting,"* *"dramatic,"* or *"too sensitive"* cut deeply for a survivor. Swap them for empathetic phrases: *"I know this feels heavy for you"* or *"Let's work through this together."*
- **Use humility to build, not tear down.** Ask questions like: *"What did you need in that moment?"* or *"How can I support you better next time?"* These humble postures of curiosity replace the need to "win" with the goal of connection.
- **Pray with humility together.** Invite God into your marriage not just with requests, but with admissions of need: *"Lord, we don't always*

get this right. Teach us to love with gentleness and humility." Shared prayer reminds your spouse that imperfection is part of growth, not rejection.

When you embody humility as the supportive spouse, you dismantle the lie that vulnerability equals danger. Instead, your actions tell your partner: *"You don't have to prove yourself here. You are already enough. I'm not keeping score—I'm keeping covenant."*

Chapter Five – Surrendered Pride: Walking in Mutual Respect

Pride often wears a convincing disguise in marriage. It shows up as defensiveness when we don't want to admit we're wrong, as silence when we refuse to ask for help, or as control when we need everything done our way. On the surface, pride looks like strength, but in reality, it builds walls where God intended bridges.

Surrendering pride doesn't mean becoming weak—it means choosing respect over rivalry, connection over self-preservation. It's the willingness to say, *"I don't have to win this argument to win your heart."* It's admitting fault when we'd rather justify ourselves or serving without expecting applause.

Scripture reminds us: *"Don't be selfish; don't try to impress others. Be humble, thinking of others as better than yourselves. Don't look out only for your own interests, but take an interest in others, too"* (Philippians 2:3–4, NLT). In marriage, pride is a barrier to healing and intimacy, especially when past wounds are present. Laying it down is an act of faith because it places the marriage into God's hands instead of our own. When both partners surrender pride, respect becomes the rhythm of the relationship, and each spouse finds freedom—not in control, but in trust. This heart posture clears the way for each partner to faithfully pursue their God-given responsibilities, loving and honoring one another with humility.

In the story of Sarah and Hagar (Genesis 16), Sarah reveals how pride can drive us to step outside of God's timing. Faced with barrenness and the pressure of her advanced age, Sarah determined to "make God's promise happen" by giving Hagar to Abraham as a surrogate. Her pride whispered, "I will do it on my own." But when Hagar conceived and began to taunt her barren mistress, Sarah lashed out, treating Hagar so harshly that she fled.

On the run, Hagar encountered the angel of the Lord, who reminded her that God saw her pain. Jehovah El Roi—the God Who Sees—acknowledged her suffering, instructed her to return and submit, and promised that her son, Ishmael, would also have many descendants because he was Abraham's child.

The takeaway is twofold: First, pride in marriage often leads us to take matters into our own hands, creating conflict rather than trusting God's timing. Sarah's inability to wait on the Lord put her at odds not only with God but also with Abraham and Hagar. Second, God never overlooks the hurt caused by prideful actions. He sees the wounded heart, calls us to humility, and invites us to stop living for ourselves. In marriage, this means avoiding harshness or malicious teasing that wounds the other. Playfulness can foster intimacy, but pride-driven words or actions tear down. True humility waits on God and seeks to honor both Him and one another.

The Wife God Was Calling Me to Be

Pride often shows up in subtle but destructive ways—especially in the desire to always be right. It's not just about winning the argument, but about needing the last word, needing to prove a point. That drive can turn small disagreements into big battles. Here's one moment when we saw this play out in our own marriage. There we were in our rent house. We had just finished arguing about the finances. As an aside, we moved nine times before we bought our first house. Until then, we lived in rent houses that would make your skin crawl. It can wear on a person's nerves to live in such conditions, especially as the family grows. Marty wanted me to work so we could buy a house. I wanted to stay home with our baby. I was content to keep slumming it, but Marty was done with that lifestyle.

My dysfunctional childhood family continually raised their voices at each other when arguing, and because we tend to follow the example set before us, I ashamedly admit that I continually raised my voice at Marty in the early years. I slammed and banged things in my fury.

"I have to get out of here for a while," Marty sighed. He took our one-year-old son with him to the store in our central Texas town north of Austin. It seemed like no time at all that they had been gone when a lady from our church frantically knocked on our door. I opened up to find all the blood drained from her face, her voice shaking as she spoke.

"Sandy, get in the car with me, now! There's been an accident. They've taken Marty and the baby to the hospital."

In those moments, shock sets in and people find it hard to think and function in a quick and rational manner, but I did the best I could. There wasn't even time for tears. We arrived just as the ambulance was bringing Marty in. The baby wasn't with him. I froze in my tracks. I loved my husband dearly, but I couldn't find our baby in anyone's arms, and I was terrified. I rushed to Marty's side as he lay on a gurney with a neck brace, and I brushed his hair from his forehead. "Don't do that, sweetie," our church friend urged. "He has glass in his hair and he'll get cut."

"Marty," I spoke through tears, "I love you."

He moaned.

"Marty," I tried again, "where's the baby?"

"He's right here and doing fine," my mother-in-law said as she walked over to where we were. She had our son on her hip.

I looked up at the doctor beside her who came to assist the paramedics. "It's true," he nodded. "We've checked the baby from head to toe. He doesn't have a scratch, bump, or bruise on him."

They checked Marty over and determined he had severe whiplash. A police officer sat down beside me as I held our son. "Mam," he began, "are you aware that your baby was not in a car seat?"

"Yes sir," I responded. "He just turned one and is no longer required to be in a car seat." Child safety laws were not as stringent then as they are now.

"I see," continued the officer, "but the man who hit your husband and baby was drunk. Your husband had stopped so he could make a left turn onto an adjacent street. The drunk driver hit him at a high rate of speed from behind. Your husband and son shouldn't even be alive. If your son hadn't at least been strapped in with his seat belt, he wouldn't be here."

I searched the officer's face. I tried to find words, but the miracle of the moment left me speechless. I nodded through my tears and walked away. The room where they had taken Marty was nearby. I went in, put the baby down, collapsed at Marty's side, and wept on his chest. "I'm so sorry for arguing with you," I said. "And I'm so sorry this happened."

"I'm sorry for arguing with you, too," Marty said, groggy from the medicine they gave him for pain. "Let's go home."

Soon after they released Marty from the hospital, we went to see our car. It looked like an accordion with its pleats squeezed together as firmly as they could be. Our hearts sank, but we were thankful beyond words for God's protection. I began to wonder. What if our last moments together on earth were spent arguing? I had a flashback to when I was barely fourteen and argued with my grandmother about the dishes I'd left undone, and she had her massive heart attack and died. As I snapped out of my flashback, I realized that being right in my arguments with Marty didn't matter at all. I was responsible for trusting God and following Marty's lead with our finances. I knew I needed to be the wife God was calling me to be. That meant snatching the tilted halo from my brow, the one that, in my pride, I donned when I started believing I was right. I wouldn't be needing that anymore. It wasn't fair to keep forcing Marty and our child to slum it just so I could have my way.

Eventually, I learned how to select a house within our budget for us to purchase. It was a modest home for what by then was our family of four. The house had three small bedrooms and one-and-a-half bathrooms, but it served us well. I learned frugality, and we didn't owe one penny on our home upon retirement. When I humbled myself before God, He honored me. When I humbled myself before Marty, he honored me.

Pursuing Your Responsibilities

Spouse, pursuing your responsibilities is the lifeblood of a Christian marriage. Don't be the yawning, lackluster kid in the video recording of a children's choir. Be the one that makes the video go viral by wholeheartedly getting into the song. Make it easy for your spouse to be who God is calling him or her to be by doing all you can to fulfill your obligations. Individually, you and your spouse have responsibilities which are detailed in the Bible. Let's look at these responsibilities, beginning with wives. Though Titus 2 addresses women in general, see how these instructions could apply to wives.

- Live in a way that honors God.
- Do not slander others or be heavy drinkers.
- Do good and teach others what is good.
- Love the husband and children.
- Live wisely and be pure.
- Care for the home.
- Be submissive to the husband, not bringing shame on the word of God.

There are also guidelines for men (husbands) in Titus 2.

- Live wisely.
- Do good works of every kind.
- Exercise self-control.
- Be worthy of respect.
- Have sound faith.
- Be filled with love and patience.

The wife's responsibility to be submissive is equally as important as the husband's responsibility to be worthy of respect. A Christian wife can easily submit to her husband's position as head of the home because her Lord Jesus is the head of the church and gave Himself for the church. However, she struggles greatly with this when the husband flies into a rage and demeans her. The husband's responsibilities are to be loving, patient, and exercise self-control, the exact opposite of flying into a rage and demeaning his wife. When he demonstrates the afore-mentioned three qualities, he proves himself worthy of respect. He makes it easy for the wife to abstain from slandering her husband, and from dishonoring God by her behavior.

Summary

In marriage, pride often disguises itself as strength—whether through defensiveness, silence, or control—but it only builds walls where God designed bridges. True strength is found in humility: choosing connection over rivalry, service over self-justification, and respect over self-preservation. Scripture calls us to value others above ourselves (Philippians 2:3–4), reminding us that surrendering pride is not weakness but faith—entrusting our marriage to God's hands.

At the same time, husbands, and wives each carry God-given responsibilities in Christian living, and these callings are the lifeblood of a Christian marriage. They enable each spouse to grow into who God is shaping them to be—teaching the husband to be worthy of respect, and the wife to honor God and her husband through her conduct. When pride is laid down and humility embraced, God provides the strength to walk in these responsibilities. As each spouse humbles themselves before God and one another, respect becomes the rhythm of their relationship, and God Himself brings honor and blessing to the marriage.

Chapter 5 questions:

Reflect on the questions below about the affect pride has had in your marriage. Use the space provided to capture your thoughts. Discuss them with your spouse if you both agree.

In what ways does pride most often show up in our marriage—through defensiveness, silence, or control? How do these behaviors affect our connection?

When was the last time I felt the need to "win" an argument with my spouse? Looking back, what mattered more—the argument itself or the health of our relationship?

How do I respond when my spouse points out a fault or weakness in me? Do I listen with humility, or do I react with pride?

In what areas of our marriage might we be trying to "make things happen on our own," like Sarah with Hagar, rather than waiting on God's timing?

What words, tones, or habits of mine have the potential to wound rather than build up? How can I replace them with words and actions that honor my spouse?

Where in our marriage do we need to surrender control and choose connection instead of rivalry?

How does Philippians 2:3–4 challenge me personally in the way I treat my spouse? What would it look like if I truly lived out those verses daily in our home?

When I think about the possibility of life being fragile and uncertain, what arguments or points of pride suddenly feel less important?

How do humility and respect make it easier for us to live out the responsibilities God has given each of us in marriage?

If our children or close friends were to observe the way we handle conflict, what would they learn about pride, humility, and trust in God?

Titus 2 Responsibilities in Practice

For Wives
- What does it look like in my marriage to live in a way that honors God in how I speak to and about my husband?
- When I'm frustrated, do I slip into gossip, sarcasm, or criticism? How might I replace those responses with respect and encouragement?
- Am I loving my husband and children in the way that makes them feel most secure, or only in the ways that are easiest for me?
- When I resist my husband's leadership, is it out of discernment—or out of pride and control?

For Husbands
- Do my daily choices reflect wisdom and long-term vision for my family, or am I more often chasing what feels good in the moment?
- Would my wife say I make it easy or difficult for her to respect me, and why?
- In moments of anger, desire, or stress, am I mastering my impulses—or letting them master me?
- When my wife disappoints me, is my first response irritation or love? What does my reaction reveal about the heart of Christ in me?

For Both
- How often do I think about my spouse's spiritual growth compared to my own comfort or needs?
- Which responsibility from Titus 2 feels most natural to me, and which one feels most costly? How might God be asking me to lean into the costly one as an act of obedience?
- If Christ asked me today, "How have you lived out My Word in your marriage?" what concrete evidence from this past week could I show Him?

Trauma Awareness: Surrendered Pride

For trauma survivors, pride is often about *self-protection* and not about arrogance. Pride can mask the vulnerability that some survivors feel: *"If I admit I need help, you'll see my weakness"* or *"If I surrender, I'll be hurt again."* For the non-traumatized partner, they may see their spouse's pride and react in frustration—wanting the survivor to "just get over it" or pushing their own way instead of listening. Healing begins when both spouses choose humility and mutual respect over control.

Tool 1: "Presence, Help, or Space?"

Instead of assuming you know what your spouse needs, ask directly:

- *Do you want me to just sit with you right now (presence)?*
- *Would it help if I do something practical (help)?*
- *Do you need some time alone (space)?*

This simple question dismantles pride because it shifts the focus from "my way" to "your need."

Tool 2: The Humility Pause

When conflict flares, both of you should pause and ask yourself:

1. *Am I trying to prove I'm right, or am I seeking to understand?*
2. *Am I protecting my spouse's dignity or defending my pride?*
3. *How can I show respect in this moment, even if we disagree?*

Write these on a card or note in your phone to use during heated moments.

Exercise 1: Serve First Day

Choose one day this week to intentionally put your spouse's needs ahead of your own—without announcing it or expecting recognition. For the traumatized spouse, this models safe, humble love. For the non-traumatized spouse, it reinforces respect for the survivor's pace of healing.

Exercise 2: "Swallowing Pride" Journal

Each spouse privately journals about one recent moment where pride got in the way of connection. Then, at an agreed time, each shares what they wrote aloud. This builds vulnerability and trust, while showing the courage it takes to admit shortcomings.

Exercise 3: Mutual Respect Statements

End your day by telling each other:

- One thing you appreciated about your spouse today.
- One way they made you feel respected.
- One way you want to show respect tomorrow.

This reorients the marriage away from competition and toward unity.

Trauma Support Applications

- **Ask, don't assume.** Use the *"Presence, Help, or Space?"* tool instead of deciding for your spouse what they need in the moment. This models humility and respect.

- **Defer to dignity.** When your spouse shuts down, resist the urge to press or lecture. Protect their dignity by giving them time and circling back gently.

- **Own your part.** Even if the conflict feels one-sided, acknowledge where your pride showed up (tone, words, body language). Humility opens the door to reconciliation.

- **Serve first.** Look for one way today to anticipate your spouse's needs without being asked. This breaks the cycle of pride by choosing action over entitlement.

- **Celebrate vulnerability.** When your spouse risks honesty about a fear, memory, or struggle, affirm it. Saying "Thank you for sharing that with me" goes further than trying to fix it.

Paul writes: *"Since God chose you to be the holy people he loves, you must clothe yourselves with tenderhearted mercy, kindness, humility, gentleness, and patience. Make allowance for each other's faults, and forgive anyone who offends you. Remember, the Lord forgave you, so you must forgive others. Above all, clothe yourselves with love, which binds us all together in perfect harmony"* (Colossians 3:12–14, NLT).

This passage paints the picture of what surrendered pride looks like in marriage. Pride demands its own way, but love wrapped in humility makes room for mercy, forgiveness, and patience. When each spouse chooses to lay down pride, they step into the rhythm of respect and create space for love to bind them together in harmony.

Surrendering pride is not the loss of self, but the gain of unity. It clears the path for husbands and wives to faithfully pursue their God-given responsibilities—walking hand in hand, clothed in humility, and bound together by the perfect harmony of Christ's love.

Chapter Six – Honoring your Spouse: Lifting Each Other Up

One of the deepest longings in marriage is to feel valued. Respect has a way of breathing life into the heart of a husband, just as love and gentleness steady the spirit of a wife. When either of those is missing, dishonor creeps in. It may not come through open betrayal—it can show up in sarcasm, criticism, or speaking poorly about your spouse to others. Dishonor slowly chips away at the foundation of intimacy.

Scripture gives us a different picture. "For wives, this means submit to your husbands as to the Lord. For a husband is the head of his wife as Christ is the head of the church… For husbands, this means love your wives, just as Christ loved the church. He gave up his life for her" (Ephesians 5:22–25, NLT). Submission and leadership are not chains—they are roles designed by God to bring balance and honor to the marriage. When a wife honors her husband's leadership, she reflects trust in God's design. When a husband lays down pride and leads through sacrificial love, he shows Christ's honor toward His bride, the church.

Honoring your spouse means making the deliberate choice to lift them up instead of tearing them down. It's about choosing words that heal rather than wound, and actions that build rather than belittle. Publicly and privately, honor strengthens the marriage covenant, making it a safe place where love can grow.

Submission Is Strength

To wives, 1 Peter 3:4-5 says, "You should clothe yourselves instead with the beauty that comes from within, the unfading beauty of a gentle and quiet spirit, which is so precious to God. This is how the holy women of old made themselves beautiful. They put their trust in God and accepted the authority of their husbands."

As I mentioned in chapter two, ladies, nothing takes my husband's breath away like my submission. Though it takes much more strength to keep my mouth shut than to fly off the handle, I would rather expend the energy. It would have made all the difference in our marriage and childrearing if I had learned this decades ago.

In Judges 16, we read that though Samson is a Nazarite, he falls in love with Delilah, a pagan Philistine. The Philistine rulers promise to give Delilah 1,100 pieces of silver if she can learn the source of Samson's strength so they can capture him. Delilah agrees. Three times she asks Samson to tell her the secret of his strength. Samson lies to her each time, escaping the Philistines' traps. He dons his tilted halo and tries to assert his will over Delilah while indulging his own desires, but she dons her tilted halo and manipulates him, nagging him day after day. Finally, he reveals his Nazarite vow and that if his hair is cut, he will lose his strength. Delilah shares Samson's secret with the Philistine rulers. They pay Delilah, and, with her help, they shave seven locks from Samson's head. When Delilah awakens him, Samson realizes Delilah's deceit. The Philistines gouge out his eyes and imprison him. When his hair grows back, he asks God for strength once more to avenge the Philistines and die with them. A young servant leads him to the temple where he can prop himself between two pillars. As Samson pushes against the pillars, the temple crashes down on everyone, killing Samson and all of the Philistines gathered there. This dynamic highlights distorted "lordship" rooted in lust and self-interest, not love or mutual respect.

"In the same way, you husbands must give honor to your wives. Treat your wife with understanding as you live together. She may be weaker than you are, but she is your equal partner in God's gift of new life. Treat her as you should so your prayers will not be hindered (1 Peter 3:7)."

Husbands, bear in mind. This reference to your wife being weaker is only physically, although she will be tempted to debate that with you if she has ever given birth! Proverbs 31 is very quick to point out all the strengths of a virtuous woman, so don't read more into the word "weaker" than what is intended. Submission is often misunderstood as weakness or silence, but biblically, it can be seen as an active expression of kindness through words, attitudes, and actions. Submission doesn't mean never speaking, but it does mean speaking with respect and kindness, even in disagreement. It shows honor to one's spouse by the tone and manner of communication. Ephesians 5:21–22: "Submit to one another out of reverence for Christ. Wives, submit to your own husbands as to the Lord." Submission here is linked to mutual service. It's an act of kindness because it considers the other person's needs and places value on their role, rather than insisting on one's own way. Philippians 2:5–8 shows Jesus humbling Himself, submitting to the Father's will—even to the point of the cross. This wasn't weakness, but the greatest act of kindness humanity has ever known. In marriage, submission echoes Christ's kindness by showing humility, selflessness, and a willingness to serve in love. When a wife practices kindness through submission, she makes it easier for her husband to respond with kindness, love, and understanding (Ephesians 5:25, 1 Peter 3:7). It is a cycle: kindness begets kindness, and submission becomes a gift that fosters gentleness and unity in the home.

What Takes My Breath Away

One of the things that takes my breath away is Marty's chivalry. I have irrational fears as a result of my childhood trauma. If I see a spider in the house, I behave as though the world is coming to an end. If Marty sees the spider first, he makes sure to kill it because he knows it will save him having to witness a complete meltdown in the long run. I've caught him doing it a few times when he thought I wasn't looking, and it indeed took my breath away.

Nothing brings tears to my eyes like Marty's understanding. I can relate to the Bible's explanation that when Rebekah became Isaac's wife, she was a special comfort to Isaac after his mother's passing (Genesis 24:67). I was raised by a man I dearly loved, my grandfather, whom I affectionately called "Daddy." When I got the call that he had passed away, I went out and swept the back porch. Marty came out, took the broom from my hands, set it aside, and wrapped me in his arms. His understanding was exactly what I needed, and it came without a word.

Grief hit hard most recently with the passing of my beloved uncle (more like a brother), the last of my family back home. My ashen face stared despairingly at the waves that crashed against the rocky cliff. I seemed not to care that they might reach the walking path on which I stood and soak me from head to toe. My heart felt like the waves, so full of hurt that it wanted to smash against something, do anything, just to make the pain go away.

Suddenly, in my spirit, a hand rested on my shoulder with a firmness and warmth that brought such comfort. The hand belonged to my heavenly Father. It pulled my shivering body back toward His strong embrace and held me as I wept against His chest. The deafening silence of my loneliness turned to the loveliest of melodies in His presence. The gnawing ache of grief became a tender bud of hope in His cradling. I knew in that moment as long as I had my Father, I could survive life's merciless blows that would otherwise have knocked me off my feet for good.

Marty could not be God to me in my anguish, but he cradled me when I returned, just as I needed him to do. There is a love that speaks for itself, carries us through the hardest of times, and takes our breath away.

As far as the instruction you are given, husbands, to honor your wives, we take this to heart. As fairytale-like as it may sound, I expect Marty to be chivalrous and ready to slay my dragons. When someone slanders me, for example, and Marty hears it, I expect him to come to my defense. No matter how strong, smart, and independent a Christian wife may seem, she longs for her breath to be taken away by a husband who honors her.

Queen Esther's Beauty

Old Testament Esther indeed had an outward beauty, but her humility, as well as her loyalty to her people, the Jews, brought the beauty of her heart to the forefront. King Xerxes had banished Queen Vashti from the palace. This was the result of her refusal to be shown off to all of the noblemen at the king's banquet. The king wanted to show her off because of her remarkable outer beauty. Upon the queen's refusal to appear, she was replaced with Esther as the new queen. In sharp contrast, it was a profound inner beauty that Esther possessed that persuaded King Xerxes to make her his queen, and later to hear her request (Esther 7:3b-4a). "I ask that my life and the lives of my people will be spared. For my people and I have been sold to those who would kill, slaughter, and annihilate us."

The king promptly grants Esther's request because of her inner beauty, a beauty that no doubt took his breath away.

The Proviso

Husbands, your instruction in 1 Peter 3:7 also comes with a proviso. If you are praying long and hard about something and aren't seeing results, examine your treatment of your wife. You can't expect God to be gracious with you if you refuse to be gracious with her.

Summary

Every marriage thrives when both husband and wife feel valued. Honor is not only about grand gestures but about daily choices—choosing words that heal instead of wound, actions that build instead of belittle, and attitudes that reflect Christ's love. Scripture calls wives to honor their husbands with respect and gentleness, and husbands to love their wives with the same sacrificial devotion Christ showed the church (Ephesians 5:22–25). This is not weakness or control, but strength expressed through humility and kindness.

Dishonor often shows up quietly—through criticism, sarcasm, or neglect—and over time, it weakens the bond of intimacy. When either spouse forgets to honor the other, it's like a halo slipping out of place: tilted by pride, selfishness, or careless words. But when humility, sacrifice, and respect are practiced, the halo is set right again, reflecting God's design for marriage.

The examples of Scripture remind us that misuse of authority brings brokenness, but humility and respect bring blessing. Honoring one another creates a safe space where love grows and faith deepens. Practiced daily, honor becomes the breathtaking beauty of a marriage where two imperfect people continually straighten each other's halos, reflecting Christ's love in the process.

Chapter 6 Questions:

Reflect on how you honor each other using the questions below. Write your responses in the space provided if you like. Discuss them with your spouse if you both agree.

In what ways do you feel most honored by your spouse—through words, actions, or attitudes?

Think of a recent moment when dishonor crept into your relationship (through sarcasm, criticism, or neglect). How did it affect your sense of closeness?

How can you make small daily choices to "straighten your spouse's halo" when pride or misunderstanding tilts it?

For wives: What does it look like for you to practice submission as an act of strength and kindness rather than weakness?

For husbands: How can you better model Christ's sacrificial love in the way you lead, serve, and protect your wife?

Publicly and privately, how do you speak about each other? Do your words lift up or subtly tear down your spouse?

What's one specific change you could each make this week to bring more honor and gentleness into your marriage?

How does the reminder that dishonor can hinder spiritual growth (1 Peter 3:7) impact the way you view your role in honoring your spouse?

Which biblical example in this chapter—Samson and Delilah, Vashti and Xerxes, Esther and Xerxes, or Isaac and Rebekah—resonates most with your marriage journey, and why?

When has your spouse last "taken your breath away" by showing honor or understanding? How can you express gratitude for it today?

Trauma Awareness: Honoring Your Spouse

For someone who has lived through abuse, neglect, or betrayal, dishonor is often a familiar wound. They may have been shamed, belittled, or dismissed so often that dishonor feels "normal." In marriage, restoring dignity becomes a holy calling. Honor—especially when shown in public—communicates, "You are valuable. I see you. I stand with you."

Dishonor doesn't always sound like insults. It can be rolling the eyes, interrupting, dismissing opinions, or joking at your spouse's expense. For a trauma survivor, even subtle dishonor can reopen old wounds of rejection. Honoring your spouse, in contrast, becomes a way of rebuilding safety and trust.

Tool 1: The Public Defense Pledge

Decide as a couple that neither of you will speak negatively about the other in public—whether with friends, family, coworkers, or on social media. Instead, commit to defend one another's dignity. Even a simple, "That's not how I see my spouse" can change the tone of a conversation.

Tool 2: The Honor Inventory

Privately list three ways you may have dishonored your spouse in the past month (tone, neglect, comparison, words). Then, ask forgiveness. Follow up with three ways you want to show honor in the coming weeks.

Exercise 1: Five Statements of Respect

Write down five specific things you respect about your spouse. Share them aloud, one at a time. For survivors, hearing respect spoken directly helps to rewire the inner script of "not enough" that trauma often plants.

Exercise 2: The 24-Hour Honor Challenge

For one full day, intentionally affirm your spouse in small ways: Thank them for a daily task, compliment their efforts, or acknowledge their character. Avoid sarcasm, criticism, or one-upmanship. At the end of the day, reflect together on how it felt to be intentionally honored.

Exercise 3: Honor in Action

Choose one way this week to lift your spouse up publicly:

- Speak well of them in front of children, family, or friends.
- Share a story of their strength or kindness.
- Defend them if someone questions their motives unfairly.

For a survivor, this can be profoundly healing—hearing your spouse affirm you in front of others is often the opposite of what they experienced in the past.

Trauma Support Applications

When your spouse carries wounds from the past, honor is one of the most powerful ways you can help rebuild what was torn down. As the supportive partner, you have the chance to model Christ's tenderness by protecting your spouse's dignity, both in private moments and in the public eye. The following applications will help you practice intentional honor so that your marriage becomes a safe place where respect, trust, and love can flourish.

- Guard your words. Refuse sarcasm or belittling, especially in public. Choose affirmations that build dignity instead.
- Lift in front of others. Intentionally praise your spouse when children, friends, or family are present.
- Defend quickly. If someone speaks ill of your spouse, respond with respect and loyalty.
- Notice the small things. Thank your spouse for everyday efforts—meals, chores, listening, or simply showing up.
- Model Christ's love. Remember that honor is not flattery—it's reflecting how Christ treasures His bride, the church.

Paul instructs believers: "Love each other with genuine affection, and take delight in honoring each other (Romans 12:10)."

In marriage, this delight means more than polite words. It is choosing to lift your spouse up in private and in public, even when stress or pride tempts you otherwise. Honor restores dignity where trauma once stripped it away. It strengthens the bond between husband and wife, reminding each that they are cherished, defended, and valued.

When spouses consistently honor one another, they echo Christ's own love—a love that sacrifices pride, protects dignity, and delights in lifting the other up.

Chapter Seven – Selflessness: The Joy of Putting Us Before Me

Selflessness in marriage is more than a humble heart—it is a humble choice. Humility shapes our attitude, teaching us not to boast or demand our own way, but selflessness takes that attitude and puts it into action. It is the daily decision to put "us" before "me," to look for ways to serve your spouse even when it costs you convenience, comfort, or preference. Where humility says, "I don't have to be first," selflessness says, "I choose you first." In this chapter, we will explore how selflessness builds joy and unity in marriage, drawing from the examples of Boaz and Ruth's devotion and the strength that comes from building a faith-filled community around your relationship.

The Overwhelming Qualities of Boaz and Ruth

Earlier, in Chapter 2, we saw how Boaz and Ruth modeled kindness—Boaz noticing Ruth's unseen sacrifices, Ruth responding with gratitude rather than entitlement, and both affirming one another's value in gentle ways. But their story also teaches us something deeper than kindness: it shows us the selflessness that makes love lasting.

Ruth's selflessness is clear from the moment she chooses to leave her homeland. Her vow to Naomi—"Where you go, I will go; your people will be my people, and your God will be my God" (Ruth 1:16)—was more than words of loyalty. It was a decision to give up the comfort of family, the security of familiar surroundings, and the possibility of an easier life. In marriage, selflessness often looks like this: laying aside personal preference or convenience to stand with the one God has placed in your life, even when the cost is high.

Boaz also demonstrates selflessness when he chooses to act as Ruth's kinsman-redeemer. Another relative had the first right to redeem Naomi's land and marry Ruth, but he declined when he realized the sacrifice required. Boaz, however, stepped forward without hesitation, willing to take on responsibility that was not required of him. He did so not because it benefited him, but because it blessed Ruth, Naomi, and ultimately the future God had written for their family. Selflessness in marriage works the same way—it often asks us to carry more than what feels fair, not because we have to, but because love compels us.

Their union shows us that selflessness is not wasted. Ruth and Boaz became part of God's larger story, their son Obed becoming the grandfather of King David, from whose line the Messiah would come. Marriage, too, is bigger than the two people in it. When we choose selflessness—when we put "us" before "me"—we step into something greater than our own desires. We create a legacy of love, one that God can use to bless generations beyond our own.

Other Biblical Examples of Selflessness

Though they faced years of childlessness and disappointment, Zechariah and Elizabeth remained faithful together (Luke 1:5-25, 57-66). When God gave them John the Baptist, Elizabeth honored Zechariah's obedience to God by insisting their son be named John, despite social pressure. Their united faith shows a shared "us before me" posture before God.

When Rebekah left everything familiar to marry Isaac, she acted with selflessness and trust (Genesis 24:62-67). Scripture says Isaac loved her deeply and she was a comfort to him after his mother's death, showing a mutual willingness to place the needs of the other above self.

Though Marty is very private and doesn't like being the topic of my writing, there is an act of selflessness that he engages in without reluctance. Like Boaz provided for Ruth, Marty makes sure I have the equipment I need to write and communicate with publishers and the public. He could use this money to buy things for himself, but he puts my desires above his own. I deeply appreciate it. His investment in my writing motivates me to put my best foot forward, both as an author and as his wife. I don't mind washing extra dishes after his meal preparation, for example, when he selflessly invests in my writing.

When Marty was a boy and a record snowfall hit the Texas and Oklahoma panhandles, his parents were unable to drive the seventeen-mile distance to check on his grandparents, whose phone was out of order. Marty's dad walked the entire distance in the snow to ensure their well-being. Our daily acts of selflessness occur when we think of others, especially our spouse, before we think of ourselves.

If the opposite of selflessness is greed, we need only look as far as Ananias and Sapphira (Acts 5:1–11). Ananias sells some property. With his wife, Sapphira, they conspire to gift the church with part of the money from the sale, but to claim the gift is the full amount. Then, they will keep the rest, and it's easy for us to imagine them with tilted halos for what, in reality, they want others to believe is their generosity. When Ananias follows through with this scheme, Peter realizes what has taken place. He points out that Ananias could have done whatever he wanted with the property and the money, but to lie was a lie to God. With that, Ananias falls down dead. It's easy to imagine his halo dropping to the floor. A few hours later, Peter confronts Sapphira about the full price for the property. We can envision her instinctively touching her head to ensure her tilted halo is still there for all to see. When she claims the full price is what they gave to the church, Peter accuses her of lying to God. Like Ananias, she too falls down dead, and again we can imagine her halo dropping to the ground. Rather than encouraging each other to remain honest and exercise selflessness, they work together to deceive the apostles. Their story shows how selfishness corrodes trust and ends in destruction.

Imagine how different the results would have been if Ananias had told Sapphira that times would be lean, but the sale of the property and the full donation to the church was what God laid on his heart to do. With Sapphira's support and their mutual trust in God to supply their needs, their act of selflessness would have been such a blessing to the church and to each other. Their straightened halos would have been crowns of reward granted by God. Matthew 6:4 says, "Give your gifts in private, and your Father, who sees everything, will reward you." Imagine the ending if Sapphira hadn't given Ananias her backing in keeping part of the money. She could have been the one to encourage Ananias to trust God and do what was right. Sometimes, fear that we won't be able to make ends meet if we comply with God's request causes us to behave selfishly or dishonestly.

We hadn't been married long when I decided to surprise Marty with a briefcase for his birthday. There was another male teacher at the school where Marty taught who had a very handsome briefcase, and I wanted Marty to carry one just as nice. Since I wasn't working and money was tight, I went to a pawn shop to trade in some of our valuables for cash. When I was buying the gift, I was giddy with anticipation to see the look on Marty's face as he opened it. I expected him to be so pleasantly surprised. Naturally, parting with our valuables at the pawn shop left a lump of sadness in my throat, but I swallowed hard and did it because Marty's happiness meant more than our valuables.

When Marty unwrapped the briefcase, his initial response was of pleasant surprise. He really needed a briefcase to carry his paperwork to and from his job. However, when he learned where I got the money for it, he was upset that I didn't check with him first. Since he grew up as a preacher's kid and knew what it was to do without, he had strong feelings about being looked down upon for not having money. He communicated feelings of inadequacy and disrespect like those he experienced in his youth from the condescending stares of others, feelings that washed in like the ocean's tide. My visit to the pawn shop had stirred up those feelings.

As we talked through the events that had unfolded and the feelings associated with them, we were able to sort out facts from fallacies. I explained that I wanted to surprise Marty with something nice for his birthday. It was never my intent to make him feel disrespected or to cause feelings of being looked down upon to resurface. It never occurred to me that my visit to the pawn shop would make him feel that way. He expressed his appreciation for my thoughtfulness in such a gift, noting my selflessness in putting one of his needs above my own. He gratefully kept the briefcase and used it until it wore out. In marriage, trauma can be complicated, but honesty and transparency facilitate trust and the healing of old wounds. Philippians 2:3-4 says, "Don't be selfish; don't try to impress others. Be humble, thinking of others as better than yourselves. Don't look out only for your own interests, but take an interest in others, too." Laying down our wants for our spouse is the true meaning of selflessness. It encompasses giving of ourselves for or to our spouse, and thinking about how our spouse feels about that giving in the context of their history.

Laughter: A Symbol of Joy

Sometimes that "joy of putting us before me" is found in the most unexpected places. One morning, I let the dogs out. At the time, we lived in farming country in the Texas panhandle, 1,500 miles from the beach city where I was raised. Frogs frequented our fenced-in back yard, secreting a substance in our dogs' mouths if the canines dared capture the amphibians. That's what I thought happened when I called the dogs into the house.

Corgi number one came in with a milky-white substance dripping from her jowls. Within moments, I heard a vocal tone that is reserved only for the greatest of panic.

"Sandy!" Marty shrieked. "What have you done?"

"Me?" I responded. "I didn't have that frog in my mouth?"

Marty retorted, "You dumb old city girl! You let the dog jump in bed with me! She's been sprayed by a skunk! Don't you even know a skunk when you smell one?"

I defended myself. "I just thought the odor was from a stout frog."

"Where's the other dog?" Marty asked. I remembered we still had one more Corgi outside. When I opened the back door, she too came in dripping with skunk spray. Kudos to the skunk for its uncanny aim from the other side of the fence.

If you've ever experienced anything like this, you know how much work goes into trying to get the skunk smell out of, well, everything. The vet gave us some spray to help with that. The carpet shampooers came and treated our carpets. The washer and dryer were in operation from morning till night.

The next day, I had to give a state assessment at the school where I taught. I didn't know my newly acquired odor was following me. "Get out!" the secretary exclaimed upon my entry into the building. "You're leaving a trail!" The odor wasn't too difficult for Marty to manage because he was retired and doing contract work from home, but I was still employed full-time. There was nothing I could do but take a little time off from work as I waited for the odor to dissipate, which it finally did.

This was an opportunity for both of us to tilt our halos and defend ourselves and our pride, but we chose to put each other first and accept the situation for what it was: a funny little story that still brings so much laughter to our family now. Laughter is a symbol of joy. It is so desperately needed when life leaves us unable or unwilling to breathe.

Selflessness and What It Means to Build a Community

Selflessness does not stop at the walls of your home. When you and your spouse choose to put one another first, that same spirit naturally extends outward, shaping how you engage with others. A self-centered marriage isolates itself, but a selfless marriage recognizes that God designed us for community. Just as Ruth and Boaz's union blessed not only themselves but the generations to come, your willingness to invest in others—sharing time, hospitality, and encouragement—becomes an act of selflessness that strengthens both your marriage and the community around it.

The marriage of Aquila and Priscilla is one of partnership (Acts 18:1–3, 18, 24–26; Romans 16:3–4). They work side by side as tentmakers and ministry partners. Though the apostle Paul isn't married, he knows the importance of building a community. Aquila and Priscilla travel with Paul, risk their lives for him (Romans 16:4), and disciple Apollos together (Acts 18:26). Their marriage reflects unity in mission and a selfless "us before me" attitude, always serving the church together. They acknowledge that a selfless marriage doesn't isolate itself, but engages in community.

Marty and I moved quite a bit in our first ten years of marriage, which is not a financially sound thing to do. However, the one thing we did right was that we built a community. We surrounded ourselves with people who shared our faith. These were the people we hung out with when we weren't furthering our education or working. We ate together, enjoyed music with each other, and spent time watching our kids play together. In addition to working in church together, we prayed with one another and encouraged each other in the Lord.

What a Community Does

Down through the years, we've been blessed with a community around our marriage. We've seen each other's kids grow up and have kids of their own. We've attended the weddings, funerals, and baptisms of one another's family members. We've enjoyed church camps together, too. We've laughed with each other till we couldn't breathe, and we've cried with each other when words wouldn't come.

Revert to Introvert

It is my opinion that my years of abuse in childhood produced my shyness, since documents surrounding my early childhood describe me as anything but shy. The foster home that I was in between my abandonment and my grandparents obtaining legal guardianship of me labeled me as a baby who knew no stranger. The foster parents took me on errands and let my outgoing personality captivate everyone I came in contact with. It seems that it wasn't until the combination of childhood sexual abuse and starting school at my strict Christian school that my personality changed and shyness set in. In addition to these factors, my grandfather worked long hours, and my grandmother didn't drive. They couldn't drop what they were doing and drive the 25 mile-distance I lived from my classmates so I could have play dates. Thus, I didn't have much interaction with children outside of school. The exception was a brief mingling with kids at church on Sunday mornings, most of whom attended public school.

It's easy for me to revert to my introverted ways. I have to force myself to make eye contact with others. I can spend long periods alone without realizing how much time has passed since I've interacted with anyone outside my family. People need to know that they're cared about and that they matter. If you're an introvert like me, ask God to take you out of your comfort zone and across someone's path. He will fill you with selflessness and make you a blessing in that person's life. While it's important to have your relationship with God be a solid one, it's also important for you to lead others into that relationship. We are blessed most when we become a blessing to others.

Few Things More Precious

You and your spouse will discover that there are few things more precious than a community built around your marriage. As you surround yourselves with people who share your faith, they will work together with you in ministry, enjoy spending time with you and your family, hold you up in prayer, and encourage you in your faith. It isn't mere coincidence that the first miracle Jesus performed was at a wedding, an event where people selflessly come together to show support for the institution of marriage.

Summary

Selflessness in marriage is a deliberate choice lived out day by day. Humility sets the tone by reminding us we don't always have to be first, but selflessness takes the next step by saying, "I choose you first." In a world that pushes self-interest and independence, marriage flourishes when we lay aside convenience or comfort to serve one another. It's in the daily choices—big and small—that we show our spouse love that puts "us" before "me."

Let the kindness of Boaz and the selflessness of Ruth remind you to see the best in each other throughout your marriage. Find the ways in which your spouse is trying to support the marriage. If your spouse isn't being supportive at all, remember that your devotion to God may be what leads your spouse to commitment or renewed commitment to God. The wife's submission makes it easy for the husband to be a team player. When the husband selflessly loves his wife, he makes it easy for her to care for him.

Chapter 7 Questions:

Reflect on the questions below about how you can show selflessness in your marriage. Use the space provided to capture your thoughts. Discuss them with your spouse if you both agree.

When was the last time you put your spouse's needs above your own, even when it cost you something? How did it affect your relationship?

In what areas of your marriage do you find it easiest to be selfless? Where is it hardest? Why do you think that is?

Think about Boaz and Ruth. Ruth gave up her homeland for Naomi and later for Boaz, while Boaz stepped in as a redeemer though it required sacrifice.

How can their story inspire the way you and your spouse approach sacrifice in your own marriage?

How do you respond when your "halo tilts"—when selfishness or pride sneaks in? What could help you realign your heart more quickly toward selflessness?

Looking at the example of Ananias & Sapphira, what warning does their story give about how selfishness can hurt intimacy and faith?

Do you and your spouse see yourselves as partners in a bigger story, like Boaz and Ruth whose legacy blessed generations? If so, what kind of legacy do you hope to build together?

How can you create rhythms of selflessness in the everyday—whether it's in chores, finances, parenting, or communication?

What role does community play in encouraging selflessness in your marriage? Who around you helps lift you up in faith and keeps your marriage strong?

When have you felt most loved by your spouse's selflessness? How can you express gratitude and encourage more of those moments?

If you were to finish this sentence honestly: "I tend to put 'me' before 'us' when…"—what would you say? How could you invite your spouse into that struggle for growth?

Trauma Awareness: Selflessness

For many survivors of trauma, the instinct to withdraw is strong. Isolation can feel safer than trust, because past experiences taught them that closeness often leads to pain. But marriage cannot thrive in isolation. Selflessness calls both partners to step outside of their comfort zones—not just for each other's sake, but also for the sake of building a community of support around their marriage. For the survivor, this means learning to risk connection again, slowly and in safe settings. For the supportive spouse, it means practicing patience and understanding, willing to put aside their own preferences in order to gently help their partner re-engage with others. Selflessness is not about losing yourself; it is about giving of yourself in ways that bring healing, stability, and shared joy.

Tool 1: Safe Network Builder

Create a list of people and places where both partners feel emotionally safe. Begin with trusted individuals or small groups, and expand slowly as comfort grows.

Tool 2: Boundary Check-In

Before committing to social events, ask the survivor: "Does this feel safe? What would help it feel safer?" Respect the answer, even if it means saying no.

Tool 3: Shared Giving Plan

Choose a way to serve together (like hosting a meal or volunteering) that allows the survivor to set the pace. Selflessness is built as you give, not just receive.

Trauma Exercises

Exercise 1: Plan a "Spouse's Day" – Dedicate one day fully around your partner's comfort and joy. Survivors learn that their needs matter; supportive spouses practice selfless action.

Exercise 2: Step Toward Community – Identify one safe couple or family to spend intentional time with this month. Keep it simple (a meal, coffee, or shared activity). Reflect afterward on how it felt.

Exercise 3: Us Before Me Reflection – At the end of the week, each partner writes one moment where they put "us" before "me." Share these aloud as a way of celebrating small acts of selflessness.

Trauma Support Applications

- Lead with patience. Allow your partner to engage at their own pace—don't rush social interactions.
- Model safety. Be the first to extend warmth and respect to others, showing your spouse what safe connection looks like.
- Check in gently. Ask how your spouse feels before, during, and after group settings. Listen without judgment.
- Share the load. When building community feels overwhelming, take on practical tasks (hosting, logistics) so your spouse can focus on connection.
- Affirm effort. Celebrate small steps, like agreeing to meet with one trusted friend, as victories of courage and growth.

Paul writes: "Don't look out only for your own interests, but take an interest in others, too" (Philippians 2:4, NLT). Selflessness in marriage begins with putting your spouse's needs above your own, but it doesn't end there. God calls couples to live beyond themselves, investing in the lives of others. For trauma survivors, this may feel risky, but each small step toward community becomes an act of healing. For the supportive spouse, every patient gesture of encouragement becomes an act of love. Together, selflessness transforms marriage from a closed circle of two into a light that blesses others, just as Ruth and Boaz's selfless choices blessed generations to come.

Chapter Eight – Calm Spirit: Responding Instead of Reacting

By now, we've seen how patience teaches us to slow down and recognize our spouse's triggers, and how humility helps us lay down pride, so we don't crush each other's spirit. But even with patience and humility, there will still be moments when emotions run hot and conflict rises. That is where a calm spirit becomes essential, because love is not easily angered (1 Corinthians 13:5). A calm spirit doesn't ignore the problem or pretend nothing is wrong; it chooses to respond with gentleness instead of reacting with anger. It's the steady presence that keeps an argument from spiraling, the soft word that diffuses tension, the quiet strength that reminds your spouse, "I am for you, not against you."

Recently, we were nearly home from a nine-hour drive. Our vacation was a lovely one, but with our two dogs in tow and our aging bodies experiencing the physical toll of the drive, we'd had enough. I wanted to get off the interstate at the more remote exit to avoid having to weave in and out of truck traffic. Marty wanted me to take the exit that would get us home the fastest. Instead of calmly explaining that our quicker path home wasn't worth my poor driving from my fear of trucks, I exploded. I yelled my objection and pounded my fist on my lap. This caused Marty, feeling completely disrespected, to yell in response. He was sick a lot as a child, and while other boys were learning to fight with their fists, Marty learned he could fight very well with his words. Thus, in our vacation argument, he donned his tilted halo and said things he didn't mean, giving full account of my past failures. He ignored 1 Corinthians 13:5. "It (Love) does not demand its own way. It is not irritable, and it keeps no record of being wronged."

He deeply hurt my feelings, causing me to withdraw. I reached to adjust my halo when, just as I predicted, the big-rig-filled exit Marty insisted that I take was treacherous. Thankfully, though, we made it home. The accomplishment of the trip in drawing us closer together seemed to be shattered in one fell swoop. We waited until the next morning to confront the obvious, allowing our tempers to cool, our bodies to rest, and our hearts to reflect. Marty has a tendency to think that when I withdraw and become silent, I'm pouting because I didn't get my way, or I'm giving him the silent treatment as a form of punishment.

Actually, my silence is my go-to place when I'm overwhelmed, a place I discovered in childhood by not being allowed to talk about emotions. Marty and I apologized to each other, acknowledging the difference a calm spirit would have made in our argument. Time to rest, reflect, and pray enabled us to adjust our halos and straighten the tilt. That morning taught us the truth of Proverbs 15:1, "A gentle answer deflects anger, but harsh words make tempers flare." Neither of us wanted to lose the progress we had made in our relationship. Psalm 65:10 says, "You drench the plowed ground with rain, melting the clods and leveling the ridges. You soften the earth with showers and bless its abundant crops." Just as God softens hard ground with rain, so can He soften our hearts until a calm spirit becomes instinctive.

Reactive Anger in the Bible

In Numbers 20, we find how reactive anger costs Moses entry into the Promised Land. Though not a story of a married couple, it perfectly demonstrates God's instruction on the consequence of reactive anger rather than a calm spirit. Moses leads the Israelites into a place in the wilderness where there's no water for them or their livestock to drink. The people complain vehemently. Moses seeks the Lord and is instructed to speak to a certain rock which will produce water. Clearly angry with the people, Moses accuses them of being rebels. He implies that if God has so miraculously brought them this far, what makes them think He can't just as miraculously take them all the way to the Promised Land? In his anger, instead of merely speaking to the rock as God directed, Moses hits it twice with a staff. An abundance of water pours out from the rock and the people (and the livestock) drink all they want. However, because Moses doesn't perform the miracle God's way, he is not allowed to lead the people into the Promised Land. A parallel can be drawn between this story and James 1:19–20. "Understand this, my dear brothers, and sisters: You must all be quick to listen, slow to speak, and slow to get angry. Human anger does not produce the righteousness God desires."

A Calm Spirit

Though we giggle about it now, we couldn't find anything funny about it at the time. Our son and daughter-in-law were packing to move. With a baby on the way, they needed a bigger home. I was spending the weekend at their house to help them pack. Our son startled me when he called me more loudly than usual. "Mom, two squares!"

"What?" I questioned. Ladies, at the risk of being sexist, why do men think we can make sense of their stunted sentences?

"You can only use two squares of toilet paper when you go to the bathroom," our son explained. "The old plumbing in this house won't allow any more." He was furious that he had to take the time to try and solve the newly risen plumbing problem while meeting his moving deadline. He slammed and banged and lectured. I apologized, but he was too worked up to hear it.

"I'm leaving," I told our daughter-in-law through tears.

"Is that what you really want to do?" she quietly asked. Her calm demeanor put me at ease. It did the same for our son.

"I'm feeling disrespected and unappreciated," I explained

"I'm sorry," our son responded. "I'm so tired and frustrated. The plumbing problem was the straw that broke the camel's back. Mom, I didn't mean to disrespect you. We appreciate everything you've done."

Without our daughter-in-law's calm spirit mediating the situation, the outcome would have probably been a different one. Her relaxed but caring tone gave me pause, allowing me to reflect and identify my feelings. Her calmness made it possible for there to be constructive dialog and consideration of each other's feelings.

In one of my favorite stories in the Bible, the prophet Elijah receives the ministry of a calm spirit in a wondrous way (1 Kings 19). Convinced that he's the only prophet of God left, and knowing Jezebel seeks to destroy him, too, he runs to the wilderness. He collapses and asks God to let him die. After angelic ministry supplies him with rest and nourishment, God has Elijah stand on Mount Sinai. There he witnesses a fierce windstorm, an earthquake, and a fire, but God isn't in any of these. Finally, Elijah hears a gentle whisper, God's calm spirit. God assures him he isn't alone, that 7,000 prophets are waiting in the wings. Elijah is revived and able to continue the Lord's work.

We see the power of a calm spirit again, albeit temporarily, when the shepherd boy, David, is summoned to play his harp for King Saul (1 Samuel 16). The tormented king is soothed as young David plays and sings psalms, and is able to continue his duties as king.

There's nothing like the Lord's demonstration of calmness when we are feeling the worst about ourselves. The gospels tell us that Peter was nervous when he denied knowing Jesus (just prior to the crucifixion). Talk about survivor's guilt. However, after the resurrection, the women at the tomb are instructed by the angels to go tell the disciples, including Peter, that they will find Jesus in Galilee (Mark 16:7). Jesus lovingly wanted Peter to know he was forgiven.

Summary

Since we know that God is love (1 John 4:8), we rely on Him to love our spouse through us. We trust Him to help us exude that same calmness of the gentle whisper, soothing melody, and splendid forgiveness of old.

Even the strongest marriages face moments when emotions run high. Love isn't proven by never getting angry; it's shown in how we handle that anger when it comes. A calm spirit steadies the heart long enough to let grace have the first word. Calmness is the posture that says, "I choose peace over pride." It's what allows us to pause before reacting, to listen before defending, and to love even when our feelings want to lead. I learned this truth again on a long drive home after a tiring trip, when exhaustion and fear collided with frustration—and calmness was the one thing we both forgot to bring along.

Tired and tense, Marty and I disagreed about which way home was best. Instead of calmly sharing my fears, I reacted in anger, and his sharp words cut deeply in return. What could have been a small disagreement grew bigger because neither of us chose calm. The next day, after rest, we apologized and realized how different the moment could have been if we had remembered Proverbs 15:1: "A gentle answer deflects anger, but harsh words make tempers flare."

Scripture also shows us the cost of reactive anger. In Numbers 20, Moses struck the rock instead of speaking to it as God commanded. Though water flowed, his anger kept him from entering the Promised Land. James 1:19–20 reminds us why: "Be quick to listen, slow to speak, and slow to get angry. Human anger does not produce the righteousness God desires."

Just as rain softens hard ground (Psalm 65:10), God can soften our hearts until calmness becomes our natural response. A calm spirit is not weakness—it's Christ's strength showing up in our words, our actions, and our love.

Chapter 8 Questions:

Reflect on the questions below about acknowledging and fostering a calm spirit in your marriage. Use the space provided to capture your thoughts. Discuss them with your spouse if you both agree.

How do you see patience, humility, and calmness building one another in a healthy marriage?

When you hear "love is not easily angered" (1 Corinthians 13:5), what does that look like in your relationship?

Think of a recent disagreement. Did your response lean more toward calmness or toward anger? What difference did it make?

When your spouse is upset, what helps you stay gentle instead of reactive? How do you personally tend to respond when you feel overwhelmed—withdrawal, words, silence, or something else? How does that affect your spouse?

In the road trip example, both spouses reacted out of frustration rather than calmness. Can you recall a time when fatigue or stress made small conflicts bigger in your marriage? What could you do differently next time?

How does it feel when harsh words are spoken in anger? Conversely, how does it feel when a gentle answer defuses tension?

Proverbs 15:1 says, "A gentle answer deflects anger, but harsh words make tempers flare." How might you intentionally practice this verse the next time conflict arises?

Moses' anger in Numbers 20 kept him from experiencing the fullness of God's promise. What "promised land" in your marriage could be at risk if anger is allowed to control your responses?

James 1:19–20 urges us to be "quick to listen, slow to speak, and slow to get angry." Which of these three is hardest for you to practice, and why?

What does a "calm spirit" look like in your marriage? Can you name one specific change you'd like to make in the way you respond to conflict?

How can you invite God to soften your heart, like rain softens the ground (Psalm 65:10), so that gentleness becomes more natural in your marriage?

Trauma Awareness: Calm Spirit

For many survivors of trauma, anger in marriage feels more threatening than it does to others. Raised voices, harsh tones, slammed doors, or even sharp sighs can trigger memories of past abuse or neglect. Their nervous system may go on high alert, interpreting anger as danger. In these moments, the survivor may shut down, withdraw, or react defensively—not because they want to, but because their body is protecting itself. That's why a calm spirit is so critical in trauma-affected marriages. When one spouse stays steady and chooses gentleness over reactivity, they create safety. Calm doesn't mean ignoring conflict. It means addressing it with emotional control, so healing can continue instead of being derailed.

Trauma Tools

- 10-Second Breath – In conflict, pause to inhale for 4 counts, hold for 2, exhale for 4. This slows the nervous system and reduces reactivity.

- Anger Signal Plan – Create a nonverbal signal to indicate when one partner feels anger rising, like touching your hand to your stomach, where we often feel that rise. This allows you to step back before words escalate.

- Time-Out Agreement – Decide on safe, respectful ways to take a break when conflict feels too heated. Promise to always return to the conversation within a set time frame (e.g., 30 minutes).

Trauma Exercises

For the spouse who has experienced trauma, practicing calm responses can feel like climbing uphill. Old wounds may tell you that anger always leads to danger, and your body may want to react in ways that feel protective. But learning to pause, breathe, and respond gently is part of your healing journey. Each time you choose calm over reaction, you teach your nervous system that this relationship is different—it is safe. These exercises are not about perfection but about progress, building the confidence that you can face conflict without fear and that peace can grow even where pain once lived.

1. **Calm Presence Practice** – Spend 5 minutes daily sitting quietly together, focusing on slow breathing. This helps the survivor's nervous system learn safety in calm togetherness.

2. **Rehearse Gentle Responses** – Role-play common conflicts (finances, chores, parenting) and practice using soft answers instead of sharp retorts.

3. **Reflective** Journaling – Each spouse journals one time during the week when they reacted instead of responded. Share with each other how it could have been handled with calm.

Trauma Support Applications

When a spouse carries the weight of past trauma, anger in the present can feel like a return to old wounds. That is why the role of the non-traumatized partner is so vital. You become the steady anchor in the storm—the one who models calm, provides stability, and creates a safe space where your spouse can trust that anger will not lead to harm. Your presence, tone, and patience all communicate, "You are safe with me." By choosing steadiness over reactivity, you help reframe conflict as partnership instead of threat, and you give your spouse the dependable foundation they need to keep healing.

- Stay steady. Keep your voice calm and body language open, even when emotions flare.
- De-escalate. Use gentle words ("I want to understand" instead of "You always…").
- Respect space. Honor time-outs without chasing or demanding immediate resolution.
- Reassure safety. Say aloud, "I'm not against you. I'm here with you." This helps reframe conflict as partnership.

- Model recovery. If you lose your temper, apologize quickly. Showing humility in anger repair builds trust.

Scripture tells us: "A gentle answer turns away wrath, but a harsh word stirs up anger" (Proverbs 15:1, NLT). Love is not easily angered because love knows that harsh reactions fuel division, while gentleness restores connection.

In trauma-affected marriages, this truth carries even greater weight. Survivors need calm presence to assure them they are safe. Supportive spouses reflect Christ when they choose steadiness instead of outburst, mercy instead of accusation. A calm spirit is not weakness—it is strength under control, the very character of Jesus. When you respond instead of react, you create the kind of marriage where peace grows, safety is restored, and love has room to flourish.

Watch out:

A gentle tone can sometimes be misunderstood by a trauma survivor as sarcasm or mockery, especially if they have experienced belittlement in the past. To avoid this, let your calm words be matched with genuine compassion, steady body language, and validation. Gentleness is about being sincere, coming to your spouse in love.

Chapter Nine – Forgiveness: Clearing the Ledger

Forgiveness is one of the hardest commands in Scripture, yet it is also one of the most freeing. In marriage, forgiveness keeps the heart from becoming weighed down by old offenses. Without it, every new disagreement is colored by the memory of past wrongs, and intimacy suffers. But forgiveness isn't just about our spouse. For those carrying trauma, forgiveness often extends to people from the past who caused deep wounds. To forgive does not mean to excuse the wrong or erase healthy boundaries. It means releasing the grip that hurt has on your heart, entrusting justice to God, and refusing to let bitterness define your future. In marriage, forgiveness allows couples to move forward without dragging the chains of yesterday into today. In life, forgiveness is the doorway through which healing begins.

When life knocks the wind out of you, forgiving those who have caused you trauma enables you to renew your commitment to God and be healthy and whole. I remember a time when I was a kid, and I slipped as I was stepping out of the bathtub. My stomach landed on the side of the tub, knocking the wind out of me. I tried to call for help, but I couldn't find any breath for a bit. Life is like that sometimes. It will knock the wind out of you. However, if your marriage is built on faith in God, He will help you find the power of love to forgive, a power that permeates the walls of pain. Your relationship with your spouse cannot be whole until you make peace with your past.

In 1 Chronicles 4:9-10, we really aren't given much of a story about a man named Jabez. His name is given to him because his mother suffers greatly with him in childbirth. I would have changed my name, but Jabez keeps it. He grows to be the most righteous one among his brothers. He asks God to bless him, be with him, enlarge his territory, and keep him from trouble. God gives him all that he asks for.

Like Jabez, I knew what it was to have a mother who could only focus on the burden of her baby. I was the fourth of my birth mother's children that she abandoned. She suffered childhood sexual abuse from the same friend who abused me, only she was not believed when she reported it. As a result, she grew to be an alcoholic, went in and out of relationships, and struggled to care for her children.

I had a foster mother appointed by the state after my abandonment and prior to my grandparents being awarded custody of me. She wrote dozens of letters to my grandmother. So many years of my life were wasted dwelling on the contents of such letters and resenting my birth mother for something that wasn't her fault. I despised her for allowing my younger siblings to be so horribly abused by the monsters that were their father figures, abuses that I witnessed on their visits to my childhood home.

The straw that broke the camel's back was when she attended the same Bible college I had. It was when our oldest child was just a baby. My birth mother fell down a small flight of stairs, drunk. For years, I was furious with her for that. It was Marty who reminded me that if it hadn't been for God's grace, I would have lived the life she lived. She has since passed, having made her peace with God. The last time I saw her, I could no longer put up the façade of self-righteousness. I collapsed, weeping and repenting at her feet in front of her wheelchair. She cupped my face in her hands, smoothed away my tears, and said, "All is forgiven."

My relationship with Marty couldn't be whole until, like Jabez in a sense, I made peace with my past. When renewing your commitment to God and to your spouse, ask God to fill your heart with love. Revisit the part of 1 Corinthians 13:5 that says, "Love keeps no record of being wronged." Trust God to guide you in forgiving those who have wronged you. You can't be whole unless you forgive them. Pray to live honorably despite your circumstances. Petition God to enlarge your territory full of hearts with whom you can share your testimony. You and your spouse will be amazed at God's response.

Something Amiss

In 1 Samuel 1:8b, it's easy for us to imagine Elkanah with his tilted halo proudly displayed as he says to his wife Hannah, "Why be downhearted just because you have no children? You have me—isn't that better than having ten sons?" What a great segway into our next marriage principle: You can't be God to your spouse.

I met Marty, a preacher's kid, at Bible college. He had been editor of his church newsletter and his church's youth leader. I had attended Christian schools for all of my schooling except the last two years of high school, and church since age five. We both had a relationship with God prior to our marriage. Times of a lack of peace were not due to each other per se, but rather something amiss between us and God.

Hannah Forfeits Her Comforts

Referring to we who follow God, in his Bible commentary on the story of Hannah, Matthew Henry says we have forfeited our comforts . In 2 Corinthians 4:12, Paul further explains that we do this to be able to relate to what others are going through and lead them to the Lord. "So we live in the face of death, but this has resulted in eternal life for you."

Hannah no doubt knew that living for God meant there would be times of rugged hardship. It wasn't that she didn't love Elkanah deeply, but he could never be what God was to her. Elkanah could have avoided the trouble had he not gone against God's plan for marriage from the beginning, that a man have only one wife. Despite the other wife's cruel treatment of her for being barren, Hannah didn't allow the seed of resentment to take root. In the pain of being barren, she refused to be bitter toward God. In the pain of cruel treatment, she refused to be bitter toward Elkanah's other wife. She allowed God to birth forgiveness in her heart. She also yearned to honor God by bearing a son that would remain in temple service throughout his life. Hannah's sincere devotion to God and forgiveness were rewarded, she gave birth to her son Samuel, and she faithfully returned her child to God for a lifetime of service. Thus, Hannah was probably able to relate to others struggling with resentment because of what she'd been through.

Time to Focus

I was only eighteen and Marty was twenty-one when we were married, with our immaturity and baggage in tow. The night before our wedding, I was feeling run down and congested. Marty offered me a decongestant, but I refused it because I wanted to be able to think clearly. He tried again more assertively, and again I refused. Marty felt disrespected and unappreciated. With nerves already on edge from the wedding only hours away, he snapped. He tried to force the pill into my mouth, smearing its blue-green coating on my pursed lips. I jumped up from a sitting position and told him the wedding was off. I ran outside and wept, pouring my heart out to God in disbelief and disappointment.

After we'd both had time to cool down, Marty found me. His eyes were just as swollen from crying as mine. He doesn't drink, so I knew his tearful apology wasn't alcohol talking. I explained that because I saw too many monsters in my childhood physically abuse my birth mother and little siblings, I couldn't be married to a man who would do that to me. It was as though I could feel my halo sliding into the tilted position. I had to dig down deep to forgive him and reach to straighten my halo, heeding the instruction in Colossians 3:13 to "Make allowance for each other's faults, and forgive anyone who offends you. Remember, the Lord forgave you, so you must forgive others." However, along with my forgiveness, I had to set a boundary to protect myself and my heart. As we knelt to pray, I told Marty that if he wanted to proceed with the wedding, he would have to make a promise to me before God not to abuse me. He has kept that promise to this day.

The Key to Resolving Conflict

This chapter is about forgiveness. In a marriage, a key step in resolving conflict is forgiveness. Lose the judgment, leave that for God. See your spouse through God's eyes, forgive them before they even know they need to ask.

"But my spouse behaves in a way that is morally reprehensible!"

"You have no idea how deeply my spouse has wounded me."

"How dare my spouse be able to get away with this!"

These thoughts may have crossed your mind. We often don a tilted halo to justify the belief that we don't need to forgive because of what has happened to us. I'm not excusing your spouse's behavior. I'm asking you to straighten your halo and fall to your knees, either figuratively or literally, and pray like you've never prayed before for your spouse. Pray like that for yourself. Your prayer (which you can change to fit your spouse's gender) might sound something like this:

"Father, I lay my wife at the foot of the cross. Show her that her temper doesn't bring You glory. Calm her, Lord. Soften her heart to desire repentance. Help her to deal with the challenges of her many roles. Soften my heart as well and forgive me if I have not been as supportive of her as I needed to be. Show me what I can do to make her job easier. Help us love each other and be the union You've called us to be. In Jesus name, Amen."

There is no need for you to take matters into your own hands. Granted, prayerfully carrying your relationship to the cross takes work and practice, but it is the key to resolving conflict. Vengeance belongs to God, not you. You can't drag your spouse kicking and screaming to repentance against his or her will. God doesn't even do that. Rather, His specialty is melting a heart of stone. Seek that, and God will give you the desire of your heart.

Summary

Forgiveness is so crucial in healing. If your marriage is built on faith in God, He will help you find the power of love to permeate pain and forgive. Extend forgiveness to your spouse and others. Your marriage cannot be whole until you make peace with your past. Ask God to fill your heart with love, for love keeps no record of being wronged. In marriage, as in serving God, you may have to forfeit your comforts. Instead of allowing the seed of bitterness to take root, allow God to birth forgiveness in your heart, just as Hannah did. Be ready to forgive each other's faults. Protect your heart with boundaries. Pray with your spouse in seeking forgiveness and renewed commitment to your spouse and to God.

Chapter 9 Questions:

Reflect on forgiveness and how it can shape your marriage. There are multiple questions for this chapter as forgiveness is a critical element of love and healing. You can choose the questions you relate to the most, or choose to respond to them all. Use the space provided to capture your thoughts. Discuss them with your spouse if you both agree.

When you read that love "keeps no record of being wronged," what emotional reaction rises first—relief, resistance, fear, or hope? Why do you think that is?

How do past offenses (even small ones) tend to resurface in your marriage? Do they come up in your thoughts, your tone, or your reactions?

What does "clearing the ledger" look like in practical terms for you? What habits—spoken or unspoken—still keep an old record alive?

Think about a recent disagreement. Were you responding only to that moment, or did your reaction include pain from earlier wounds?

When you picture releasing the hurt versus holding it, which feels safer? Which feels more vulnerable? Why?

Like the story of Jabez, are there parts of your past that you've carried into your marriage—wounds, labels, or memories—that still shape the way you love today?

What relationships from your past (family, caregivers, abusers, authority figures) still affect how quickly or slowly you forgive in the present?

How might forgiving someone from your past change the way you show love to your spouse?

Which part of your story still feels like "it knocked the wind out of me"? How might God be inviting you to breathe again through forgiveness?

When has forgiveness in your marriage required strong boundaries—not as punishment, but as protection?

Do you tend to confuse forgiveness with excusing behavior, erasing consequences, or pretending something didn't hurt? What truth do you need to remind yourself of?

In what situations do you forgive quickly, but without healing? Where do you forgive slowly, but deeply? What might help you learn a more balanced rhythm?

Think of a moment when your spouse asked for forgiveness (or showed it through action). What helped you believe their sincerity? What helped restore trust?

Hannah released bitterness toward God and the cruelty of her rival. Which of those is more difficult for you—forgiving God for what He allowed, or forgiving people for what they did?

Elkanah couldn't take the place of God for Hannah. Where might you be expecting your spouse to heal a pain only God can tend?

What prayer (like the example prayer for a spouse) could you begin praying over your marriage when forgiveness feels impossible?

As you reflect on the story at the birth mother's wheelchair, what does it stir in you about the power of last-minute healing?

What does it stir in you about forgiveness that comes too late to speak— but not too late to free your heart?

When conflict arises, are you more likely to replay past hurts, withdraw emotionally, or retaliate? What pattern do you see?

How does your spouse typically seek forgiveness—through words, touch, acts of service, changed behavior, or prayer? How can you better recognize their attempts?

What small grievances do you tend to collect—tones, habits, comments, expectations—and how do these "little ledgers" affect your closeness?

What would a true "fresh start" look like in your relationship this week? What one thing could you both do to symbolize it?

How has trauma shaped your understanding of forgiveness? Does forgiving feel dangerous, disloyal to your pain, or like letting someone "get away with it"?

In what ways can forgiveness become part of your healing—not just reconciliation with your spouse, but restoration of your own heart?

What part of your past are you afraid to face because forgiveness feels too painful? What would it look like to ask God to go there with you?

When you consider the "Burning the List" exercise in the trauma section, what specific memory, hurt, or phrase would you need to place on that list?

How can you gently communicate to your spouse when you need forgiveness and when you need boundaries, without confusing the two?

What step of forgiveness could you take today that would lighten your spirit, even slightly?

Trauma Awareness: Forgiveness

Forgiveness is never simple. You may have heard people say, "just forgive and move on," but words like that do little to touch the depth of a wound. In marriage, and especially in the life of a trauma survivor, forgiveness does not mean excusing hurt or allowing abuse to continue. Forgiveness is about releasing the power of the wrong so it no longer controls the present. The first step is being honest about the pain. Give yourself permission to say how the hurt made you feel. Healing begins when you let yourself feel the anger, the grief, or the betrayal that pain caused. Then, take those raw emotions and lay them before God. Place the weight of it all into His hands. Only then can you begin to let go and walk into true forgiveness. Forgiveness is not forgetting, and it is not the loss of healthy boundaries. Forgiveness is courage—it is trusting God with justice and choosing to keep your heart free from the ledger of wrongs. In marriage, forgiveness opens the door for growth. It makes space for love to flourish without dragging yesterday into today.

A Biblical View of Boundaries

When we speak of boundaries, we are not talking about selfish walls or excuses to withhold love. Boundaries are the God-given lines that help us guard what He has entrusted to us—our hearts, our bodies, and our spirits. Scripture tells us, "Above all else, guard your heart, for everything you do flows from it" (Proverbs 4:23). Jesus also said, "Out of the abundance of the heart, the mouth speaks" (Matthew 12:34). What fills your heart will eventually flow out into your words, your tone, and your actions. Guarding your heart through healthy boundaries keeps bitterness, resentment, and anger from spilling into your marriage.

For a trauma survivor, boundaries are especially important. They may mean limiting harmful patterns, saying no to unsafe behavior, or stepping back until trust is rebuilt. Boundaries do not weaken forgiveness; they make forgiveness possible. By protecting what is tender and holy in your heart, you create the space for God to heal you and for love to grow in a safe, life-giving way.

How to Set Boundaries God's Way:

- **Pray for wisdom.** Ask the Lord to show you what needs protecting and how to speak truth in love (James 1:5, Ephesians 4:15).
- **Speak with clarity.** Use simple, honest words to explain what you need, without accusation.
- **Stay consistent.** When your actions align with your words, trust grows.
- **Act with gentleness.** Boundaries are not ultimatums. They are invitations to walk in love without crossing into harm.
- **Leave room for growth.** As healing happens, God may expand the capacity of your heart, softening what once felt too tender to touch.

The Intent of Boundaries:

- To create **safety** where love can flourish.
- To bring **clarity** so both spouses know what is honoring and what is not.
- To affirm **dignity** because every person bears the image of God.
- To protect **unity** because love cannot thrive where wounds are constantly reopened.

Boundaries do not weaken forgiveness; they make forgiveness possible. They prevent repeated harm and create the space where trust, respect, and healing can take root.

<u>**Trauma Tools**</u>

- **Boundary + Forgiveness Matrix** – Draw a simple grid: one side for "Forgiveness Given," the other for "Boundaries Needed." This reminds couples that forgiving doesn't mean re-opening the door to harmful behavior.

- **Release Prayer** – Speak aloud a prayer that releases the offender into God's hands: *"Lord, I choose to forgive ____. I release them from my judgment. Justice belongs to You, not me."*
- **Ledger Check** – Ask yourself: "Am I holding onto this mistake in my memory as evidence? Or have I released it?" This helps expose hidden scorekeeping.

Trauma Exercises

1. **Burning the List** – Write down lingering grievances from the past. Pray over them together, then burn or shred the paper as a symbol of release.
2. **Fresh Start Ritual** – At the end of each week, take a moment to affirm: *"I forgive you for the ways you hurt me this week. I release it and choose to start fresh."*
3. **Forgiveness Journal** – For survivors: Write one painful memory and then write a prayer of release beneath it. This keeps forgiveness specific and intentional.

Trauma Support Applications

When your partner carries wounds from the past, forgiveness can be one of the hardest steps in healing. Old hurts cling tightly, and letting go may feel like losing the protection that pain has provided. This is where your role as the supportive spouse becomes vital. You can help create an environment where forgiveness feels possible by offering steadiness, compassion, and prayer. Your spouse needs to know that forgiveness does not erase boundaries and does not minimize what they endured. What they need most is to see that you respect those boundaries while encouraging them to release bitterness into God's hands. Be patient with the process because forgiveness is rarely immediate. Sometimes it unfolds slowly, layer by layer, as trust is rebuilt and old wounds are released. Your calm presence, your gentle encouragement, and your willingness to keep pointing to God's justice will help your spouse discover the freedom that forgiveness brings.

- **Don't pressure.** Forgiveness takes time; pushing for it can retraumatize.
- **Affirm boundaries.** Remind your spouse that forgiveness does not mean losing their voice or tolerating abuse.
- **Model forgiveness.** Share openly when you release your spouse's mistakes, showing that you also live by this principle.
- **Offer prayer.** Gently ask, *"Would you like me to pray with you about this?"* and respect their answer.
- **Celebrate steps.** Recognize even small acts of forgiveness as victories of healing.

Paul reminds us: *"Bear with each other and forgive one another if any of you has a grievance against someone. Forgive as the Lord forgave you"* (Colossians 3:13, NIV). Forgiveness is not denying pain—it is choosing not to let pain write the final chapter. For trauma survivors, it is the path to freedom. For supportive spouses, it is the steady reminder that God's mercy is greater than any failure. Love keeps no record of wrongs because love trusts God to handle justice, while we choose peace.

Watch Out: Forgiveness does not always mean reconciliation, especially when very tragic trauma occurs. You can forgive someone without putting yourself back in harm's way. Forgiveness is about releasing bitterness and entrusting justice to God. Reconciliation requires repentance and change and should only be attempted if the survivor feels safe.

Chapter Ten – Integrity: Loving What Is Good

"It (love) does not rejoice about injustice but rejoices when truth wins out." Love does not take pleasure in lies, manipulation, or selfish gain. It does not look for opportunities to twist the truth or hide behind half-answers. Instead, love finds joy in honesty, transparency, and trust. To rejoice in the truth is to build a marriage on solid ground, where what is spoken can be believed, and what is promised can be counted on. Integrity in marriage means living in such a way that your word can be trusted. Integrity is the quiet strength that says, *"My yes means yes, my no means no."* When integrity marks a marriage, each spouse knows they are safe—not because the other is flawless, but because their words and actions align with the truth of Christ.

Finding My Voice (Moses and Me)

One of the most beautiful portraits of integrity comes from a man who doubted his own ability to speak the truth aloud—Moses. Exodus 4:10-17 paints a beautiful portrait of humble, inarticulate Moses. The New King James Version gives the scene that Charlton Heston feel.

Then Moses said to the Lord, "O my Lord, I am not eloquent, neither before nor since You have spoken to Your servant; but I am slow of speech and slow of tongue."

So the Lord said to him, "Who has made man's mouth? Or who makes the mute, the deaf, the seeing, or the blind? Have not I, the Lord? Now therefore, go, and I will be with your mouth and teach you what you shall say." But he said, "O my Lord, please send by the hand of whomever else You may send."

So the anger of the Lord was kindled against Moses, and He said: "Is not Aaron the Levite your brother? I know that he can speak well. And look, he is also coming out to meet you. When he sees you, he will be glad in his heart. Now you shall speak to him and put the words in his mouth. And I will be with your mouth and with his mouth, and I will teach you what you shall do. So he shall be your spokesman to the people. And he himself shall be as a mouth for you, and you shall be to him as God. And you shall take this rod in your hand, with which you shall do the signs."

Notice that Moses' brother, Aaron, is there to speak the words God gives Moses. God tries to make Moses understand that He is a God of integrity. I'm crying as I write these words. Moses was not able to grow up with his mom, but he was spared while all the other baby Israelite boys were killed because his mother knew he was special (Exodus 2). In adulthood, he killed an Egyptian for beating an Israelite, then was on the run for his own life. With all the injustices in the world, it was hard to believe God would keep His word. We who lug our baggage over our shoulder tend to don a tilted halo, thinking we have a right to our skepticism because of past wounds. Once God gets in Moses' face (so to speak) and convinces Moses of His integrity, Moses humbles himself before God, straightens his halo, and accurately receives what the Israelites and Pharaoh need to hear. He isn't an eloquent speaker, but he becomes the leader God envisioned from the beginning.

Like Moses, I was so inarticulate, I never imagined that I could be a public speaker. I didn't have a speech impediment. I wasn't autistic. I didn't have Asperger's. I wasn't on the spectrum. I've taught precious students who fell into these categories, but I wasn't one of them. It was abuse that caused me to withdraw. A lady once said of me, "I've never seen a child so full of quiet."

My grandfather's position on sharing feelings became evident years later when I asked him about my grandmother's childhood. He knew very little. "She grew up in a dugout in Kansas," he began. "After she told me that, I didn't pry any more. We can assume that she grew up poor, and those things are meant to be private."

Though my grandmother died when I was barely fourteen, she lived long enough to scold me for trying to share my feelings. If I spoke of a cute boy at school, she said I was growing up "loose" like my birth mother. If I mentioned my loneliness from not having other kids to hang out with, she said I was ungrateful for what I did have. Much of what people have to say revolves around our feelings, and if we can't express those, what's the point of saying anything at all?

When my aunt began her education to become a school psychologist and advocated for me to share my feelings at home, my grandparents resented her. I've often been told their generation was a different time, but it didn't make dealing with feelings any easier for me.

There were also the feelings from the eight years of childhood sexual abuse I didn't breathe a word about to anyone. When it came to things other than my sexual abuse, I shared those feelings with my aunt, but not until my teenage years. With the sexual abuse, I reported it (after eight years) to someone I trusted, that person had me tell my grandparents, we never saw my perpetrator again, and the abuse was never spoken of again. Looking back, no wonder I was so quiet.

Much like Moses, I was thrown into the spotlight. Because I could write well, I was asked to compose speeches for special occasions in high school. When a farewell speech for a retiring teacher needed to be delivered, I was elected for the daunting task solely due to my writing ability. The teacher's cascading tears told me the speech was a success, but I hoped I never had to do that again. The next year at Bible college, I was required to introduce a song on choir tour. I grimaced. I prayed about what to say, and I felt impressed to share a little of my testimony. I penned the words with ease, but the thought of delivering them left me undone. I couldn't bear to be so vulnerable. That's when I came across the aforementioned story of Moses. I realized that my humility in God's presence was all He needed to direct the words to the hearts who needed to hear them. I shared snippets of my testimony on several occasions that year, encouraging people who, like me and maybe even like Moses, needed it.

My childhood dream was to be a writer, but the responsibilities of marriage and children told me I needed a profession that would provide a steady income, one that I didn't think writing could supply. When I became a teacher, I found that speaking in front of children was far easier than speaking to adult audiences. As far as the venue, church was my place of choice for public speaking. My secular work was as a public-school teacher, and the majority of my church work was in children's ministries. However, when you're part of a preacher's family, you become a jack of all trades in the church, so Marty and I taught adult Bible classes. While I still preferred addressing children, I became more comfortable with adult audiences.

Once I retired, I was able to travel and speak to secular and church-affiliated organizations about my work as an author and about my childhood. Now, when I double over with a panic attack right before time to speak, I remember the face of my elderly babysitter as tears trailed the creases of her timeworn face. God gave me the words to the first poem I wrote for her as a child, and when she cried, I knew writing for God's glory was what I wanted to do more than anything else in my life. I recall the tears of the teacher whose retirement speech I wrote and delivered in high school. I remember the eyes nearly swollen shut, crying people who've told me after speaking engagements that my story was their story, and my hope became their hope. I recollect the story of the humble Moses who, like me, would have given anything to hide behind a writing tool rather than address a crowd, but who still became a great leader and a witness of the very glory of God. My anxiety subsides. God saw something in me I couldn't see in myself. He straightened the tilted halo I wore when I believed I had a right to my skepticism because of my wounded past. I knew He was a God of His word. Now, I get to be His pen and His spokesperson. Life doesn't get any better than this.

I share my public speaking story to emphasize that God wants us to follow His example of integrity, an example which is even more important to follow in marriage. Marty has had to work hard to prove himself a man of integrity to me and make our marriage a safe place for me to communicate. Though I'd had a few on-stage experiences with public speaking, I found communicating difficult in the early years of marriage. When our children were very small, before I started teaching, we had regular visits with some of Marty's colleagues. I barely said two words, and if a large group was gathered, I said nothing at all. It wasn't my intention to be rude. I just shut down, completely unable to find the courage to speak. Like God, Marty never lost sight of who I could become. He knew from reading my writings that intriguing thoughts rummaged around in my brain, and he patiently engaged me in conversations and coaxed me until speaking became second nature. Thus, if I have too much gift for gab nowadays, it's actually his fault!

Once in the early years during an argument, Marty picked up a music box. I thought he was going to throw it at me, so I ran away. He got in the car and drove until he found me six blocks from home. With his imaginary halo in hand rather than arrogantly displayed on his brow, he ashamedly confessed that he picked up the music box because he was angry and wanted to smash it on the floor, but certainly not to throw it at me. He reaffirmed his vow from the night before our wedding that he would never physically hurt me. It took patience on his part to convince me that I could count on him being something my perpetrator wasn't, a man of integrity. I could talk with Marty and not be afraid.

Though he never wants to be part of the limelight, he always encourages me to answer God's call on my life. Whether investing in a writing course for me, surprising me with Bible study materials so I too can grow in integrity, managing all of my technology, or working as my cashier after speaking engagements while I autograph my books, Marty encourages me. Couples, you will rarely take your spouse's breath away more than when you, with integrity, get behind him/her 100% and cheer him/her on to follow God's leading. The impact this will have for the kingdom of God will be the greatest thing you will ever witness.

When Integrity Breaks: Adam & Eve

In Genesis 3, we find Adam and Eve being deceived by the serpent (aka Satan). They forget God's instructions not to eat of the Tree of the Knowledge of Good and Evil or they would die. Instead, their hearts accept the serpent's lie that the only reason God doesn't want them to eat from that tree is that He doesn't want them to know good and evil like He does. Eve believes the lie first and disobeys God, then she gets Adam to do the same. As soon as they sin, they feel ashamed and exposed. God confronts them. Adam shifts blame to Eve. Eve shifts blame to the serpent. As a result, the serpent is sentenced to crawl on its belly. Satan is sentenced to the Lord's destruction. Eve is sentenced to pain in childbirth and subordination to Adam. Adam is sentenced to hardship in growing crops. The couple is banished from the Garden of Eden and is sentenced to eventual death. Their relationship to God and each other is damaged. Still,

God demonstrates integrity by being true to His word and making a path to redemption. We prove integrity when we take responsibility for our failures, not in shifting blame and pretending we haven't failed.

Integrity in Marriage: Building Safe Communication

Just prior to Marty's heart stent surgery, we had a conversation. "This heart problem sure came out of nowhere," I commented.

"Well, not exactly," Marty admitted sheepishly. Seeing my confused look, he continued. "I've been having symptoms for a while, but I didn't want to worry you."

I gasped. "That's not okay. When it comes to our well-being, we have to be open and honest with each other. You breathe in and I breathe out."

The Cost of Hidden Things: Rachel's Idols

No matter how pure the intentions, a relationship built on lies, even lies of omission, creates cracks of distrust in its walls. In Genesis 31:19, Jacob's wife Rachel, without telling her husband, takes the idols (teraphim) of Laban, her father, as they are leaving his house. According to some Jewish traditions, Rachel took the *teraphim* because she wanted to keep her father Laban from idolatry.[1] This was a well-intentioned reason to be secretive. Later though, in Genesis 35, Jacob tells his family that God wants them to move to Bethel. Jacob instructs them that all of their pagan idols will need to be done away with, and that the family will need to go through a purification process. The Bible isn't clear on how the idols came into their possession, which leaves us wondering if Rachel's secret was responsible.

God sees everything anyway. He knows our thoughts and intentions (Revelation 2:23), so why try to hide them? Well-intentioned secrets in a

---

[1] ©1996–present The Enduring Word Bible Commentary by David Guzik – enduringword.com. Used with permission.

marriage can have grave consequences. That which begins as nothing more than a dirty snowflake morphs into a hideous boulder-size snowball. The harmless glance at a website you have no business perusing or the disguising of a container in your medicine cabinet as something other than the habit-forming drug within are prime examples.

My Hidden Battle: The Eating Disorder

I used to have Rachel tendencies. I wanted everything to be perfect. If that meant keeping secrets to the death, even from Marty, I'd do it. I was abandoned as a baby. I had been repeatedly sexually abused by a family friend from the ages of four to twelve. My grandmother died of a massive heart attack when I was barely fourteen. My grandfather soon remarried, and I had to move away from everything I held dear. Since I couldn't control anything in my life, I decided to control the one thing I could, my eating. The problem was that it started controlling me. In the earliest years of our marriage, I hid Ipecac syrup so I could purge between meals and stay the perfect weight. That can lead to cardiomyopathy – when the heart muscle becomes enlarged, thick, or rigid – and heart failure.[2] In the article "Ipecac - Don't Use It," it states, "When such poisoning victims got ipecac anyway, they developed serious complications or even died. More and more people with eating disorders were using ipecac to make themselves throw up. Regular use of ipecac syrup is dangerous; for example, chronic users have died from heart problems."[3]

Remain Transparent

Embracing the concept of integrity in a marriage means that you become vulnerable in places that you want to remain dark and untouched. Your spouse becomes the partner that you need to help you carry the weight

---

[2] https://www.heart.org/en/news/2024/02/26/how-eating-disorders-can-damage-the-heart
Published: February 26, 2024, How Eating Disorders Can Damage the Heart by Laura Williamson, American Heart Association News.

[3] https://www.poison.org/articles/ipecac-do-not-use-it, Internet article: *Ipecac – Don't Use It.*

of your past and support you in your healing. In holding my purging back from Marty, I felt ashamed and deceitful. Once I learned I was pregnant, I asked God to help me give up the purging habit for our baby's sake. To let go of the pain that led me to purge, I asked God to heal those wounds, and He did. He held me up by showing me that when I relinquish control to Him, He drenches me with showers of blessings. I also asked him to help me learn to be a woman of integrity and be transparent with Marty, and God granted that request. If you want to have a marriage of solid mutual trust, allow its glasslike walls to remain transparent with open and honest communication. When I was transparent with Marty and let him in, it was good not to have to feel alone anymore. I was able to share struggles I'd never shared with him up until that time. I could finally be honest with him, myself, and with God. Be transparent. Be a man or woman of your word. Love your spouse enough to be as one. When your spouse breathes in, you breathe out.

Summary

If marriage is about being open and honest with each other, a Christian marriage is even more so. A relationship built on lies, even lies of omission, creates cracks of distrust in its walls. Well-intentioned secrets can have grave consequences. Remain transparent with each other about money, sickness, temptations, everything. Function like a well-oiled machine.

Integrity is one of the most beautiful ways love shows up in a marriage. Love doesn't hide behind half-truths or twisted words—it rejoices when truth wins. I've learned that integrity is quiet but powerful. It means my yes can be trusted, my no is honest, and my words and actions match what I believe about God's character.

Like Moses, I once believed I wasn't equipped to speak. Abuse and silence had stolen my voice long before I realized how much I needed it. But God—patient, faithful, and full of integrity—taught me that He can speak through anyone willing to be honest. Over time, through His grace and Marty's gentle encouragement, I found safety in communication and learned that integrity builds the kind of trust where love can breathe.

I've seen what happens when integrity breaks. Adam and Eve's blame-shifting, Rachel's secret idols, and even my own hidden battle with an eating disorder all remind me that secrets grow in the dark until they destroy the very thing we meant to protect. Healing began when I stopped hiding. When I chose transparency with God and with Marty, shame lost its grip.

Now, integrity means living with glass walls where nothing is hidden, there is nothing to fear. It means being open about where I've been so God can use it for His glory. In marriage, it means loving with truth, speaking with honesty, and trusting that when my husband breathes in, I can breathe out. That's where love feels most like God—safe, seen, and full of integrity.

Chapter 10 Questions:

Reflect on integrity and its impact on your marriage. Use the space provided to capture your thoughts. Discuss them with your spouse if you both agree.

When you read that love "rejoices when truth wins out," what emotions does that stir in you?

How do you define integrity in your own words? What does it feel like when someone lives with integrity toward you?

In what areas of your marriage or daily life is it hardest to stay fully truthful—with your words, your emotions, or your motives?

Why do you think honesty can sometimes feel risky, even with people who love us?

How does seeing God's integrity in Scripture shape your desire to be truthful and transparent?

Moses felt unqualified to speak. Have there been moments when you've doubted your own ability to share what's inside you?

What experiences from your past—family expectations, rejection, trauma—have taught you to stay silent instead of honest?

How has God helped you find your voice again, or how might He be inviting you to do so now?

What makes it easier for you to open up to your spouse or loved ones?

In your relationship, what helps truth feel safe rather than threatening?

How does your honesty affect your spouse's (or loved one's) sense of peace and security?

Think of a time when a small lie or unspoken truth created distance between you and your partner. What lesson did it teach you?

What daily habits could help you practice "glass-wall transparency," where nothing is hidden and love can breathe freely?

What role does humility play in speaking the truth kindly instead of harshly?

Adam and Eve lost integrity through blame and hiding. When you make mistakes, do you tend to hide, blame, or take responsibility?

Rachel's hidden idols were born from good intentions. Can you think of a time when you hid something to protect someone—or yourself—and it still caused pain?

What do these stories teach you about the cost of secrecy, even when motives seem pure?

If you have experienced trauma, what has honesty come to mean for you—safety, fear, or freedom?

How does consistent truth from your spouse or friends begin to heal the places where deception once wounded you?

When was the last time honesty brought you peace instead of punishment?

Are there any areas of your life that still feel "off limits" to God? What keeps you from letting Him into those places?

What does it look like for you to live with integrity before God first, and then before others?

How might practicing honesty with God make it easier to be honest with your spouse or family?

How can your story of learning to tell the truth—about your past, your pain, or your healing—become part of someone else's hope?

Trauma Awareness: Integrity

When a person has endured trauma like betrayal, neglect, gaslighting, or abuse, the nervous system learns that truth is unsafe. Survivors often equate transparency with danger because, in the past, honesty may have led to punishment, humiliation, or rejection. So even when they long for closeness, a deep instinct whispers, "If I tell the truth, I'll be hurt or abandoned."

That's why truth in a trauma-affected marriage is more than a moral or spiritual obedience; it's a healing act. Every truthful exchange between spouses rewires the body to believe: "I can be honest and still be loved." It rewards their vulnerability with safety.

Truth dismantles suspicion because secrecy is what trauma feeds on. Lies, even small omissions, confirm the survivor's fear that people can't be trusted. But when a spouse consistently speaks truth with gentleness, their transparency becomes a safe rhythm that soothes the survivor's hypervigilance. Change doesn't happen overnight or with one honest discussion. The wounds that built that suspicion didn't happen overnight and they can't be healed that fast either. Consistent behaviors pave the way for healing.

Integrity, then, becomes more than being "honest." It's the alignment of what you say, what you do, and who you are before God. And within marriage, integrity can also manifest as respect—respecting your spouse enough to give them the truth, to follow through on promises, and to safeguard trust with consistent actions.

When truth and respect meet, suspicion loses its footing. Honesty without respect can sound like accusation; respect without honesty becomes flattery or avoidance. But integrity weaves the two together and speaks truth kindly and acts honestly even when no one is watching.

Scripture grounds this beautifully: "The Lord detests lying lips, but He delights in those who tell the truth." (Proverbs 12:22) "Love must be sincere. Hate what is evil; cling to what is good." (Romans 12:9)

Integrity is telling the truth, living it out in such a way that your spouse's heart feels secure in your words, and following up those words with actions that do what you say. Integrity restores what trauma once broke: the ability to believe someone's word without fear of betrayal. Seeing promises fulfilled helps retrain the body to expect safety instead of disappointment.

Tool 1: Weekly "Truth Check-In"

Create integrity in your marriage by fostering a safe place to be transparent and honest.

Continue the existing tool for spouses to find time together weekly. This time, share something you have avoided discussing, however small. It may be a financial detail, a regret, or an emotional truth. The purpose isn't confession for guilt's sake, but to prove that transparency leads to safety, not punishment.

Remember the tone:

- Begin with prayer. Acknowledge God's role in your marriage and that He is the Truth, the Light, and the center of your relationship.
- Focus on honesty, not accusation. This tool is not meant to lay blame, point fingers or fix a problem.
- End with affirmation. Thank each other for sharing, for being vulnerable and for trusting one another with something that you had held back.

Tool 2: The Accountability Anchor

Rebuild reliability where trauma or broken promises have eroded trust.

- **Say it Clearly** – When you make a promise (big or small), state it plainly so your spouse hears and understands the commitment. *Example: "I'll call you after work before I head home."*
- **Do it Faithfully** – Follow through. If plans change, communicate immediately.
- **Own it Honestly** – If you forget or fail, admit it quickly without excuses: "I said I would call, and I didn't. That was wrong. I'm sorry."
- **Repair it Respectfully** – Ask, "How did that affect you?" and listen without defensiveness.
- **Rebuild Consistency** – Track progress together. Small patterns of follow-through rebuild reliability and emotional safety.

Accountability is the visible proof of integrity. It says, "You can trust not just my words, but my patterns."

Exercise: Integrity in Action

This exercise brings together truth, respect, and accountability, with a goal to help couples practice consistency between what they say and what they do.

Steps:

1. Identify One Area of Follow-Through — Choose one area this week where you often make promises or declarations (e.g., finances, household chores, prayer time, emotional availability).
2. Make a Micro-Commitment — Set a small, specific goal: "I will text when I'm leaving work," or "I'll take the lead on dinner twice this week."
3. Track Together — Keep a shared list (whiteboard, phone note, or journal) of fulfilled commitments.
4. Reflect Weekly — Ask, "Did I keep my word this week?" and "How did your follow-through make me feel?"
5. Celebrate Progress — Every small step reinforces safety and trust.

Trauma Support Application:

Integrity is about safety as well as faithfulness. Inconsistent behavior, vague commitments, forgotten promises, or shifting tones can feel like the emotional ground is moving beneath the survivor's feet. Even small inconsistencies can echo the unpredictability of past trauma. That's why integrity, honesty, transparency, and follow-through—become a deep form of connection for the survivor. Following through shows respect for the survivor's need for stability and consistency. "Let your 'yes' be yes and your 'no,' no." (Matthew 5:37)

Build that consistency by practicing intentional check-ins. It may just look like "How are you feeling today," or more a deliberate ask, "How can I support you today?" Find the right way to let your spouse know that you are there for them *before* they break down and ask for your attention. Show them that your presence is consistent, not conditional.

Ambiguity is stressful for survivors. Support your spouse by declaring your plans clearly. Instead of saying, "I'll take care of that later," try, "I plan to take that trash out after dinner. If anything changes, I will let you know." That simple step eliminates guesswork for the survivor. There is no arduous effort to decipher your tone or your schedule. Clarity is transparency, and is one of the truest form of integrity.

Chapter Eleven – Protection: Creating a Safe Haven

"Love never gives up, never loses faith, is always hopeful, and endures through every circumstance." — 1 Corinthians 13:7

In marriage, protection means more than physical safety; it means creating a refuge where your spouse's heart can rest without fear. True love doesn't expose weaknesses or weaponize vulnerabilities; it stands guard over them. To protect is to say, *"Your heart is safe with me."*

The NLT passage tells us that love "never gives up." That isn't passive endurance—it's active defense. It means love refuses to quit when things get hard, refuses to turn its back when storms arise, and refuses to let harm from outsiders, temptations, or careless words invade the sacred space of marriage. Protection is love's perseverance in action.

When one spouse carries wounds from trauma, that kind of protection becomes vital. Safety must be experienced before love can be believed. Creating safety means staying steady when emotions swing, honoring boundaries, and proving with consistency that trust will not be broken. It's guarding one another's peace rather than controlling one another's choices. When love refuses to give up, it protects the relationship, not by force, but through faithfulness.

Marty and I have been on a few cruises in our marriage, but none amused us as much as our trip to Mexico. Marty remembered stories from my teenage trips across the border, when I somehow couldn't escape the attention of the young men in the shops and restaurants. Years later, as adults cruising there together, he stuck to me like glue. I found it charming—his nearness, his protectiveness, the way he stayed close without hovering. It was a quiet picture of how loved I felt.

One evening on that same cruise, a storm rolled in, and the ship began to rock with turbulent waves. I became terribly seasick, and Marty cared for me every moment. He got me water, helped me steady my steps, and stayed right by my side while the room spun. His steadiness reminded me of how love is meant to protect—not with force, but with presence. Sometimes protection is simply staying close when someone is struggling.

Some of you know what it feels like to be on a storm-tossed ship, but without anyone steady beside you. While I had Marty to lean on, you may feel like you're bracing yourself against the waves alone.

Let me speak for a moment to those of you who carry deep wounds. You're embarking on yet another voyage in life feeling abandoned and unseen. The people who should have protected you have turned away, and others have been too busy or overwhelmed to notice your pain. Nothing in you looks forward to this voyage. Death has taken the ones who would have otherwise come to your rescue. You never miss them more than at times like these. While families and friends gather with laughter and celebration, you do whatever it takes to drown out the noise. The exaggerated merriment may be in your imagination, but that doesn't keep it from taunting you as it echoes through the chambers of your heart.

But hear me now—God sees you on that ship. He knows exactly what the storms feel like, and He draws closer, not farther, when the waves rise. God knows exactly what you're feeling. If you will allow

Him, He'll be closer than ever to you just now. God never intended for the pain of the past to overtake you. The bitterness, hurt, and defeat you carry aren't part of His plan. His goal all along was to hold you when no one else would, to hear you when no one else could, and to love you like no one else has or ever will. He will help you forgive, heal, and overcome. Just as Marty stayed close to me in Mexico—protective, steady, and attentive—God stays even closer. He will help you forgive, heal, and overcome.

And here is the beautiful part: Only those who have sailed stormy seas can fully understand when other voyagers are hurting. God will use what you've endured to anchor and mentor someone else one day. The blessing He's preparing for you will be worth it.

A Bride to One Husband

In 2 Corinthians 11:2-4, Paul said, "For I am jealous for you with the jealousy of God himself. I promised you as a pure bride to one husband—Christ. But I fear that somehow your pure and undivided devotion to Christ will be corrupted, just as Eve was deceived by the cunning ways of the serpent. You happily put up with whatever anyone tells you, even if they preach a different Jesus than the one we preach, or a different kind of Spirit than the one you received, or a different kind of gospel than the one you believed."

The Lie from the Pit of Hell

There is no room in your relationship for misguided affection. Sadly, misguided affection is the very thing that plagues marriage voraciously. We all know couples whose marriage seemed to go on forever, and suddenly ended due to infidelity. Often it was a lie from the pit of hell about God's tolerance for adultery that carried their marriage to its demise.

In Genesis 39, Joseph serves as attendant to Potiphar, captain of Pharaoh's guard. Potiphar's wife becomes consumed with desire for Joseph and repeatedly tries to seduce him. Instead of keeping her interactions with Joseph in safe, accountable settings—such as speaking only when attendants were nearby—she isolates herself with him, creating secrecy and danger in her marriage.

Joseph refuses every advance, honoring both God and the trust Potiphar placed in him. Enraged by his rejection, Potiphar's wife lies and accuses Joseph of attacking her. Joseph is imprisoned, yet God rewards his integrity, eventually raising him to second in command over Egypt.

The lesson for marriage is simple but vital: Lack of boundaries creates opportunity for temptation, confusion, and betrayal—while clear, predictable boundaries build trust and emotional safety. Trauma-affected spouses especially need these boundaries, because secrecy, private meetings, or blurred lines can trigger fear, insecurity, or old wounds. Joseph illustrates that protecting a covenant sometimes requires firm "no's," transparent behavior, and choosing integrity even when it costs you. Just as misguided affection threatens a marriage from the outside, distractions threaten it from the inside.

Married couples, never put yourself in a compromising position. In education, I figured out a way to keep myself in the public eye when I was with a person of the opposite sex that was not my husband. (Marty and I worked in the same building for many years.) If I had to carpool with someone of the opposite sex, I invited another person to join the carpool. When I needed to meet with a colleague of the opposite sex, I picked a public location for our meeting, or I made the location public by leaving the door open when possible, or only agreeing to meet in a room with a window.

Avoid websites you have no business perusing like the infectious disease that infidelity is. We conquer misguided affection when both spouses pour the sand from our vial into the large container, Christ. The grains of sand are not to be separated. They remain one in Him.

Remove the Distractions

Beware! There will be those who try to pull you away, both from God and from your spouse. True brothers and sisters in the Lord will never behave in that manner, but wolves in sheep's clothing will. It is not coincidental that Paul uses the analogy of a monogamous marital relationship and a commitment to Christ (2 Corinthians 11:2-4).

When you find your attention wandering, remove the distractions. Since Marty and I both worked in education for many years, we became well acquainted with Attention Deficit Disorder. To get students to focus on the task at hand, distractions had to be removed. Spouse, you are no different. Get rid of forms of entertainment, for example, if you are tempted to let them deter you from your devotion to your spouse. Stay focused on where your devotion lies. This is just as applicable to marriage as it is to faith. In marriage, there is no point in comparison shopping because no one is perfect. The protection that love provides is the commitment to watch for distractions, wanderings, and lies that threaten the integrity of marriage.

Communicating Love (When Love Grows Cold)

Finally, be generous in communicating your love for your spouse. I can't ever remember my grandmother telling me she loved me. Because she was harsh and cruel, I interpreted her lack of affection as her not loving me. Shortly before her death, I asked her about it. "Love is something you show, not tell" she retorted.

I learned eventually that her painful past made her the way she was. She really did love me; she just didn't know how to show it. The Christmas three weeks after her passing, I found a wrapped electric typewriter from her under the tree. She wanted to support my dream of being a writer.

Children who don't experience a home environment in which genuine love is communicated struggle with this as adults. Though my grandfather told me he loved me, the love he and my grandmother shared was never verbalized or demonstrated. When it came to the way they treated each other, they each wore tilted halos, believing they were justified in the way they behaved. They slept in separate rooms and they were never affectionate with each other in my presence. They fought a great deal with loud exchanges full of profanity. What helped me learn not to behave this way with Marty, unfortunately, was seeing the demise of the marriages of people dearest to us. In most cases, the demise came because of a wandering eye when love grew cold. There is a direct correlation between love for God growing cold and love for a spouse growing cold. Read your Bible, pray, and surround yourself with people who share your faith. Strengthen your walk with God, and your marriage will follow suit.

When you are wearing the tilted halo, like my grandparents, it might make the marriage and family a less safe haven. This can easily lead to entertaining wolves in sheep's clothing. You can create a safe haven for your marriage by establishing a loving home in which your spouse and children feel loved, safe, and protected. Review this book's chapters on kindness, selflessness, and forgiveness, and practice them in your home. Love that builds a safe haven for your family includes removing the distractions and misguided affection to ensure pure devotion to your spouse, regularly communicating genuine love to your spouse and children and acceptance of them when things don't go well, and committing to endure even when things get hard or painful.

Summary

Protection in marriage is not merely guarding against physical harm—it is creating a refuge where each spouse's heart feels secure. Love that "never gives up" stands watch over the relationship with steady faithfulness, setting healthy boundaries, resisting misguided affection, and removing distractions that pull the heart away from devotion. Just as Joseph honored God by refusing secrecy or compromise, couples protect their covenant by choosing transparency, accountability, and integrity.

For spouses touched by trauma, this protection becomes even more essential. Emotional safety, predictable behavior, and gentle communication reassure the wounded heart that it will not be abandoned or mocked. A protected marriage is not built through control, but through consistency. It is strengthened when both partners speak love generously, guard each other's dignity, and keep Christ at the center of their unity.

When you eliminate the influences that divide, remain faithful in your boundaries, and devote yourselves to nurturing a safe and loving home, you create a haven where healing can flourish, and love can endure through every circumstance.

Chapter 11 Questions:

Reflect on protection's role in your marriage. Use the space provided to capture your thoughts. Discuss them with your spouse if you both agree.

When you read that love "never gives up" (1 Corinthians 13:7), what does that kind of protective love look like in your marriage today?

In what moments do you feel most emotionally protected by your spouse? How do those moments strengthen your trust?

Are there areas where your spouse may not feel emotionally safe with you? What might help restore safety?

Think of a time when you felt vulnerable. What did your spouse do—or what could they have done—to protect your heart?

What temptations, relationships, or habits have the potential to weaken your devotion to your spouse?

How do you personally define healthy relational boundaries? Are there any boundaries your marriage needs to strengthen?

Have you ever found yourself in a situation—online or in person—that could have been misinterpreted or felt unsafe to your spouse?

What steps can you take to make your interactions with the opposite sex consistently transparent and above reproach?

How does the story of Joseph challenge you to choose integrity even when it's inconvenient or misunderstood?

What "distractions from the inside" (entertainment, comparison, busyness, attention drift) threaten your connection with your spouse?

What "distractions from the outside" (other people's influence, social media, workplace pressures) steal your emotional focus?

How can you intentionally remove or limit those distractions for the sake of your marriage?

Do you find yourself comparing your marriage to others? How does comparison erode protection?

How do you usually communicate love when tensions rise? Does your spouse receive it as protection—or as withdrawal?

Are there words you need to begin saying more often—"I love you," "I appreciate you," "I'm listening"—to strengthen your spouse's sense of safety?

What does it look like for you to actively "guard your spouse's peace" when they're overwhelmed or hurting?

If you or your spouse carries trauma, what moments feel most threatening or destabilizing in conflict or stress?

Which of the Safe Haven elements—physical safety, emotional safety, spiritual safety, relational safety, predictability—needs the most attention in your home?

How can you become more consistent in your tone, responses, and follow-through so your spouse knows they are safe with you?

What boundaries or reassurances would help your spouse feel more secure during conflict or emotional overload?

In what ways are you guarding your covenant with the same devotion Paul describes in 2 Corinthians 11:2–4?

How well are you protecting your walk with God—and how does that affect your protection of your marriage?

What would it look like this week to create a deeper sense of "God is our hiding place" (Psalm 32:7) within your home?

Trauma Awareness: Protection

Protection is not about control; it is about consistency. For a trauma survivor, the feeling of being safe is often unfamiliar. Past experiences of betrayal, chaos, or neglect can make stability feel suspicious and comfort feel dangerous. When love "never gives up," it does more than endure; it shelters. It builds the kind of predictable, peaceful environment where healing can finally take root.

In a trauma-impacted marriage, protection begins with understanding that safety is both physical and emotional. It is how survivors know they can express themselves without fear of mockery or punishment. It is the tone of voice that stays gentle when emotions rise. It is the spouse who stays instead of walking away during conflict. Every consistent action whispers, "You are secure here."

God modeled this through His care for His people. Psalm 32:7 reminds us, "For you are my hiding place; you protect me from trouble. You surround me with songs of victory." (NLT) When love protects, it echoes the heart of God. It surrounds instead of exposes. It sings peace where fear once ruled. In a home marked by trauma, that protection often looks like staying soft in moments that once would have become hard.

Protection also means guarding your marriage from outside harm. For many survivors, outside opinions or relationships can trigger fear of abandonment or rejection. Setting boundaries around friends, in-laws, and technology use is not mistrust; it is stewardship. It keeps the covenant of marriage a sacred refuge, a place where both hearts can rest. Love that never gives up keeps watch. It stands between the marriage and whatever might divide it.

Tool 1: The Safe Haven Checklist

Use this checklist together to identify what safety looks like in your marriage.

- Physical Safety – Do both of us feel free from fear of physical harm or intimidation?
- Emotional Safety – Can we share our feelings without fear of mockery or retaliation?
- Spiritual Safety – Do we pray together or invite God into hard conversations?
- Relational Safety – Do we guard each other's dignity when we are with family, friends, or online?
- Predictability – Do our actions match our words, especially when emotions are high?

Review the checklist together and talk about where your marriage feels strong and where it feels uncertain. Pray over the areas that need growth, asking God to make your home a refuge of peace.

Tool 2: The Calm Presence Practice

This practice helps couples learn how protection shows up through emotional steadiness. It is about staying connected in the middle of conflict. Sometimes we need the conflict to create a space for healthy discussion.

When tension rises, pause and take one slow breath together.

- Speak one sentence that reassures safety, such as: "I am not leaving. We are okay. We will talk this through."
- Keep your tone gentle and your posture relaxed. Your calm presence helps your spouse's nervous system settle.
- Close the moment by praying aloud or placing a hand on your spouse's shoulder as a reminder of unity.

Exercise 1: Create a Safety Agreement

Each spouse writes three things that make them feel safe and three things that make them feel unsafe. Share your lists and talk about ways to meet each other's needs.

Examples:

- *I feel safe when you speak calmly even when you are upset.*
- *I feel unsafe when you walk away without explaining why.*

Once both have shared, write a short statement you can post somewhere visible:

"In our marriage, we protect each other's peace by speaking gently, staying present, and trusting God to guide our reactions."

Revisit this agreement monthly and update it as healing grows.

Exercise 2: Guard the Gate

Together, list three influences or habits that could harm your unity. This might include gossip, certain media, overcommitment, or unhealthy friendships.

Commit to guard the gate by choosing together what enters your home and hearts. Pray Psalm 32:7 aloud as a declaration of protection: "For you are my hiding place; you protect me from trouble. You surround me with songs of victory."

Trauma Support Applications

When your partner carries trauma, your role as protector is not to fix or rescue them but to provide a consistent refuge where they can heal at their own pace. Protect through presence by staying gentle when emotions surge, by listening when words are hard to find, and by keeping promises that rebuild trust over time.

Ask yourself daily, "Does my spouse feel safe with me right now?" If the answer might be no, pause and ask what reassurance or boundary would help. Avoid saying things like "You are overreacting" or "That is not what I meant." Instead, try "I can see that this feels heavy. I am here with you."

Protection is also about spiritual covering. Pray over your spouse aloud, even briefly, asking God to surround your marriage with peace. Your calm, faith-filled leadership becomes a shelter for their weary heart. Love that never gives up tells your spouse, *"You can rest here. You are safe, you are seen, and you are not alone."*

Chapter Twelve – Trust and Hope: Anchoring in God's Faithfulness

"Love never gives up, **never loses faith, is always hopefu**l, and endures through every circumstance."— 1 Corinthians 13:7

Trust and hope are the twin anchors of a lasting marriage. Trust allows love to stand firm when life feels uncertain. Hope keeps that love alive when circumstances seem impossible. Together, they form the steady ground beneath every promise you make to one another. In marriage, trust is built through truth, reliability, and consistency. It grows slowly but can be broken quickly. Hope, on the other hand, is what breathes life back into a weary marriage when trust has been shaken. Hope believes that God is still writing your story even when you cannot see the next chapter. Trust and hope walk hand in hand because you cannot truly trust someone you have lost hope in, and you cannot hold hope without choosing to trust again.

Every couple will face seasons when trust is tested and hope feels dim. There will be moments when words fall short, finances strain, or prayers seem unanswered. In those times, it is not your strength that sustains your marriage, but God's faithfulness. Proverbs 3:5–6 reminds us, "Trust in the Lord with all your heart; do not depend on your own understanding. Seek his will in all you do, and he will show you which path to take." Trust in God steadies your heart so you can extend trust to your spouse.

Hope, too, has divine roots. Romans 15:13 says, "I pray that God, the source of hope, will fill you completely with joy and peace because you trust in him. Then you will overflow with confident hope through the power of the Holy Spirit." When you invite God into the fragile places of your marriage, He fills the cracks with His strength and teaches you to believe again.

A Double Rainbow of Hope

Matthew 19:3-12 references Jesus' position on divorce. A man leaves his parents, becomes one with his wife, and the man and wife should not be separated. An allowance for divorce was made in the law because of the hard hearts of man, not because it was God's will.

In chapter one of this guide, I recounted Marty's lack of understanding of my continued struggle with childhood trauma, my inability to effectively communicate it, our frustrations with childrearing, and the impasse in our marriage that carried our family to a hotel getaway. We clung to hope in God by the tiniest thread, when, in that hotel room, the most brilliant double rainbow appeared. The sight brought us to our knees as we tearfully prayed together. We returned home knowing we'd be okay. God's promises remain. They don't crumble under pressure. We can trust them. Like the second rainbow is a mirror image of the first (but in reverse order), we should strive to be a mirror image of God.

Trusting God with All You Have

That weekend didn't magically erase our struggles, but it anchored something deep in us. If God could meet us in a hotel room at the edge of breaking, we could trust Him with the rest of our story including everything we owned, earned, and feared losing.

From the start of our marriage, Marty and I agreed that we would tithe, give offerings, and do all that we could to help those in Christian ministry. We like to do this because churches and missionaries help people in need. As we've honored God in this manner, He has continually been faithful to meet our needs.

In the early years of our marriage, I questioned Marty's decision to tithe because times were lean. We rented a house for $85 a month. It was nestled in the beautiful Ozark mountains of northwest Arkansas. Beside our home were chicken houses. The strong odor wafted through our windows, and plentiful mice scurried to and fro across our floor, but we were in love.

I suffered culture shock coming from a big city by the ocean to the strange but beautiful backwoods. I had to learn the language, like when the neighbors wanted to carry me across a narry (rhymes with starry) bridge to do my trading. Marty explained that they were offering to give me a ride over the narrow bridge to the store. When they told me to get to the cave because a storm (tornado) was coming, they weren't talking about a storm cellar or shelter. It was a real cave! I was terrified of coming face to face with a bear. Still, even with the differences in language and culture, I was happy to do life there with the man of my dreams.

I went to work to help put Marty through his last two years of college, but $3 an hour (which was minimum wage in those days) barely made ends meet. On my days off, I occasionally went to visit a lady from our church. Blue roses grew wild on her property. Their loveliness stole my breath and brought tears to my eyes. I was reminded of Luke 12:26-30, to think about the lilies arrayed in beauty. If God cares for them, how much more would He care for us? As Marty and I committed to seek God and His righteousness above all else, our needs would be met. I no longer worried about our finances when Marty put a check in the offering box.

Since children learn trust from their fathers, Marty is better at it than I am. Still, we both are finding that learning to trust God and honor Him with all we have is a process. It's a process, though, that's well worth the journey. So place your trust in God. Commit to honoring Him with all you have. Study what the Bible says about tithing. Support your home church with your time, talents, and finances. Provide the means for those in ministry to have food and shelter. You will find your own needs being met as God rewards you for your faithfulness, and for placing your trust in Him.

The Woman of Shunem

The woman from Shunem (2 Kings 4) is the epitome of trusting God. Though she and her elderly husband are wealthy, she persuades him to show hospitality to God's prophet, Elisha, in furnishing him with a place to stay every time he comes by. To bless them for their support of the ministry, God gives them a son. When the boy grows some, he gets very sick and dies. They send for Elisha, who comes and prays, and the boy is brought back to life. The Lord blesses the woman and her family repeatedly (2 Kings 8) because of her faithfulness in seeing to the needs of the ministry.

Nabal and Abigail

The Shunem woman's story is a picture of a tender, trusting heart. But Scripture also gives us a sobering opposite of someone who hardened his heart instead of softening it before God.

We see a sharp contrast in 1 Samuel 25 with Nabal, a wealthy man who is harsh and mean in all his dealings. His wife Abigail, however, is wise and gracious. When David asks for provisions for his men—men who had protected Nabal's shepherds—Nabal tilts his halo and responds with cruelty. David prepares for retaliation, but Abigail intervenes with straightened halo, generous provisions, and a humble plea, preventing needless bloodshed. The next day, when she tells Nabal what happened, he has a stroke and dies ten days later.

Imagine how different Nabal's story could have been if he had softened his heart before God and straightened his halo as his wife did. Instead, his hardness destroyed him. When we let the pressures of life harden our spirits and tilt our halos, we become like Nabal. Our relationships crumble, and everything around us begins to fall apart.

Sarah

Nabal's story warns us what happens when we refuse to trust God, but some struggles with trust are more subtle, rooted not in open arrogance, but in fear, impatience, or weariness while we're waiting on God's promises.

In Genesis 16, we learn of Sarah's struggle with trust. Though God had already promised to make an elderly Abraham the father of many nations, an elderly Sarah grows impatient waiting for it to happen. She didn't have access to all the incredible testimonies of miracle after miracle that are at our fingertips today. Jesus' Aunt Elizabeth wouldn't come along until hundreds of years later to give her testimony of miraculously birthing John the Baptist in her old age. So, in Sarah's impatience and uncertainty, she takes matters into her own hands and has Abraham marry her Egyptian servant, Hagar, a woman who can give birth to Abraham's children. Once Hagar realizes she's pregnant, she becomes cruel to Sarah. In retaliation, Sarah gets so harsh with Hagar that the surrogate runs away. An angel ministers to Hagar in the wilderness, explaining that if she submissively returns to Sarah, God will give her an infinite number of descendants. She returns and gives birth to a son, Ishmael.

Thirteen years later, Sarah miraculously becomes pregnant. Her child, Isaac, is the one through whom Abraham's descendants will be counted. When he is weaned, Isaac joins his family for a celebration.

Ishmael makes fun of him, so Sarah has Ishmael and Hagar sent away. Still, God takes care of them, preserving Ishmael's line as well as Isaac's. I just can't help but wonder how many times Sarah kicked herself for not trusting God for her miracle baby instead of arranging lineage through Hagar. Like Sarah, we may believe in God and still wrestle with how He will do what He promised.

Zechariah and Elizabeth

Even faithful people can struggle to trust that God will move in His time and His way. An example of that struggle with trust is when Zechariah learns Elizabeth is going to have a baby that will prepare the way of the Messiah (Luke 1). Zechariah asks the angel how he can know for sure this will happen, since he is old and his wife is getting there. The angel tells Zechariah that because of his lack of trust, he will remain unable to speak until his son's birth, which is exactly what happens. God takes trust seriously, yet He remains faithful even when we falter.

The Car Wash

From Shunem to Nabal, from Sarah to Zechariah, the theme is the same: God is faithful even when our trust wobbles. The question is not whether He can be trusted, but whether we will loosen our grip and let Him lead—even in everyday, ordinary moments.

Marty and I spent entirely too much time arguing about money throughout our marriage. We both had to learn to trust God with our finances. However, to this day, when it comes to trust, I can't even go to the car wash without such fear that there is weeping and gnashing of teeth! I can't bear to relinquish control to the automation requiring me to put my vehicle in neutral, take my foot off the brake, and take my hands off the steering wheel. Are they insane? I have to be in control of my surroundings at all times! Thus, I can relate to people I read about in the Bible who also struggled with putting their trust in God and securing their hope in Him. I can honestly say, though, that when Marty and I have done so, true peace has been lavished upon us.

Summary

Trust and hope are the steady anchors that hold a marriage when storms roll in. Trust teaches us to lean on God instead of our own understanding, and hope reminds us that He is still writing our story when we cannot see the ending. From the double rainbow that met our family in one of our darkest seasons to the many times God provided for us in lean years, we have learned that His faithfulness never wavers.

Every couple will face moments that test the heart—moments when childhood wounds resurface, when misunderstandings multiply, or when provision feels uncertain. But when we keep our hearts tender before God, He meets us in those places. His promises do not crumble under pressure. He has a way of taking what feels impossible and using it for good, just as He did for the Shunem woman, for Abraham and Sarah, and for Zechariah and Elizabeth.

As you grow together, choose to honor God with all you have—your time, your resources, your forgiveness, your patience, and your willingness to keep trying. Trust Him to do what He has always done: keep His word. Let hope rise in your home again. God is faithful, and when your marriage is anchored in Him, you will endure every circumstance together.

Chapter 12 Questions:

Reflect on the trust and hope that you maintain in your marriage. Use the space provided to capture your thoughts. Discuss them with your spouse if you both agree.

What does "anchoring your marriage in God's faithfulness" mean to you personally?

Which is harder for you right now—trusting God or hoping for what you cannot see? Why?

How do you usually respond when circumstances feel hopeless or uncertain?

Have you ever faced a moment in your marriage where you couldn't see a way forward?

During seasons of misunderstanding or emotional distance, what helps you feel hopeful again?

How can you reflect God's character to your spouse when things feel stuck?

In what areas do you struggle to relinquish control, much like the "car wash" moment?

How have you seen God provide for you in the past when circumstances were tight?

What practical steps can you take to trust God more fully with your resources or finances?

Do you relate more to the Shunem woman's faith, Sarah's impatience, or Zechariah's doubt? Why?

What can you learn from Abigail's straightened halo and steady wisdom in contrast to Nabal's tilted halo and hardened heart?

What small trust step is God inviting you to take this week?

If trauma affects your marriage, what actions from your spouse make trust feel safer?

Where does hope tend to fade for you, and what strengthens it again?

Is there a promise from God you need to return to and believe again?

How can you practice "holding hope" for your spouse when they cannot see it yet?

What rhythms (prayer, giving, Scripture, gratitude) can help anchor your home in God's faithfulness?

What testimony from your past reminds you that God can still make a way where there isn't one?

Trauma Awareness: Trust and Hope

For someone who has lived through trauma, trust can feel like the hardest part of love. Past betrayal, neglect, or abuse may have taught the survivor that trust is dangerous and hope only leads to disappointment. Yet God calls us to a deeper kind of trust, one rooted not in people's perfection but in His faithfulness. When love "never loses faith" and "is always hopeful," it reflects God's heart for restoration.

In a trauma-affected marriage, the survivor may wrestle with fear that trust will be broken again. Even small mistakes or forgotten promises can reopen old wounds. To rebuild trust, safety must come first, and consistency must follow. Every honest word, every kept promise, and every gentle response helps rewire what trauma once taught the heart to expect. It tells your spouse, "You can count on me. I am not leaving when it gets hard."

Hope, too, can feel fragile when life has been marked by pain. But hope is what keeps love from closing in on itself. It looks forward to what God can redeem, even when the evidence is not yet visible. Romans 15:13 reminds us, "I pray that God, the source of hope, will fill you completely with joy and peace because you trust in him. Then you will overflow with confident hope through the power of the Holy Spirit." Hope begins in the heart of God, not in our circumstances. When couples cling to Him together, they learn that hope is not a feeling to find, but a truth to hold.

In trauma recovery, trust and hope grow together like two vines that strengthen one another. The survivor begins to trust again as they experience consistency, honesty, and gentleness. The supportive spouse holds hope when the survivor cannot see it yet. Over time, God weaves these two into one steadfast thread of faith that holds the marriage secure.

Tool 1: The Trust Ledger

This tool helps couples see trust not as a single event but as a pattern of faithfulness over time.

- List Trust Builders – Write down specific actions that strengthen your confidence in each other. Examples include honesty about finances, following through on commitments, or keeping confidences.
- List Trust Breakers – Identify behaviors that damage trust, such as sarcasm, secrecy, or avoiding difficult conversations.
- Pray for Renewal – Together, ask God to reveal any patterns that weaken your trust. Commit to one change you will each make this week to rebuild confidence.
- Track Progress – Revisit your list monthly to celebrate growth. Trust is not rebuilt overnight, but it deepens with every consistent action.

Psalm 37:3 says, "Trust in the Lord and do good. Then you will live safely in the land and prosper." When couples choose to do good toward one another daily, trust becomes a shelter they both can rest under.

Tool 2: Hope Statements

Hope begins with the words we speak. When you declare truth over your marriage, you remind your hearts who your foundation really is. Together, speak these statements aloud once a week:

- "Even when I cannot see the outcome, I trust that God is working for our good."
- "Our story is not finished; God is still writing it."
- "We will keep believing in what God has promised us, even when progress feels slow."
- "We are anchored in His faithfulness, not our failures."

Speaking words of hope reinforces truth in both your hearts and trains your minds to focus on what is eternal rather than temporary.

Exercise 1: The Faithful Footsteps Journal

Each evening for one week, write down one way you saw God's faithfulness that day, even in small things. It might be a kind word, a calm conversation, or a peaceful moment. At the end of the week, share your journals and thank God together for His consistency. This practice helps train your hearts to look for signs of His steady presence rather than focusing on what is lacking.

Exercise 2: The Hope Anchor

Find a small object that symbolizes hope for you both, such as a smooth stone, a cross, or a verse card. Keep it in a visible place as a reminder that no matter what happens, your hope is anchored in God. When conflict or discouragement arises, hold the object together, pray, and reaffirm your trust in His faithfulness.

Hebrews 6:19 says, "This hope is a strong and trustworthy anchor for our souls. It leads us through the curtain into God's inner sanctuary." Hope in God anchors both your hearts to the One who never fails.

Trauma Support Application

If your spouse carries trauma, you may often find yourself holding hope for both of you. This is a sacred role. Your steadiness helps your spouse relearn that trust can be safe and that love can remain. Be patient with their fears. They are not rejecting you; they are remembering what once broke them. Every time you respond with gentleness instead of frustration, you are helping their heart relearn safety.

When your spouse hesitates to trust, avoid rushing or demanding reassurance. Simply show through consistent action that you are dependable. Follow through on what you say. Keep your promises, even the small ones. If you make a mistake, own it quickly and sincerely. Your humility will speak louder than perfection ever could.

Most importantly, keep your hope grounded in God. Pray for your spouse out loud when they cannot pray for themselves. Speak Scripture over your marriage. Remind them that God is faithful even when feelings are not. When you anchor your love in Him, your spouse will slowly begin to rest in that same strength.

Love that "never loses faith" and "is always hopeful" reflects the heart of Christ. It is not blind optimism; it is confident expectation that God is still writing redemption into your story. Trust may take time, but hope is what carries you through until it blooms again.

Chapter Thirteen – Perseverance: Holding on When It's Hard

"Love never gives up, never loses faith, is always hopeful, and endures through every circumstance." — 1 Corinthians 13:7

Perseverance is love's final and fiercest expression. It is the strength to remain when everything in you wants to walk away. In marriage, perseverance is not stubbornness; it is commitment refined by grace. It is the quiet courage that whispers, "We will get through this," when the storms feel unending.

Every couple will face seasons that test endurance. There are days when patience is worn thin, communication falters, and prayer feels unanswered. Perseverance does not pretend those moments are easy; it simply refuses to let them define the end of the story. It remembers that God is faithful, even when feelings fade and progress seems slow. Galatians 6:9 encourages us, "So let's not get tired of doing what is good. At just the right time we will reap a harvest of blessing if we don't give up."

In marriage, perseverance looks like showing up again after a hard day. It is choosing to forgive when it would be easier to withdraw. It is praying together when you would rather stay silent. Perseverance does not deny pain; it brings it to the cross and lets God transform it into purpose. Romans 5:3–4 reminds us, "We can rejoice, too, when we run into problems and trials, for we know that they help us develop endurance. And endurance develops strength of character, and character strengthens our confident hope of salvation."

Job and His Wife

The story of Job grips my heart, as I mentioned previously, because his wife finds it impossible to fight for her husband's faith in the midst of such loss. It also grips my heart because she sees perseverance as an exercise in futility. She misses the point that God has so much confidence in Job's perseverance, He allows Satan to strip them of practically everything to prove Job won't give up on Him. When Job's wife can't find anything praiseworthy about God, Job does (Job 19:25-26). Perseverance, especially in a trauma-impacted marriage, sometimes means one spouse holds the faith when the other can't. Perseverance is not giving up on prayer when pain lingers.

Hannah and Elkanah

Earlier, I mentioned how Elkanah couldn't be God to Hannah. It would have been easy for Hannah to be resentful about her polygamous marriage, her barrenness, and the other wife's cruelty. Instead, she perseveres in prayer for a child, one that can be raised in God's service, and God grants her request. In lingering trauma or pain, married couple, perseverance in prayer results in God's faithfulness.

Mary & Joseph

As was discussed before, Mary and Joseph's humility toward God was key during Mary's pregnancy, potential scandal, and the uncertainty she and Joseph faced. The prospect of childrearing can be daunting for any new parent, but for the parents of the Messiah, it could have been too frightening to attempt. Still, they persevered through relocation and danger, remaining obedient when the way was unclear. They stayed faithful to God and to each other. Perseverance in marriage means pursuing obedience together when the path makes no sense. It means choosing to obey God when others don't understand your journey.

The Hysterectomy Story

Perseverance is never only something we read about in Scripture. It shows up in our living rooms, hospital gowns, and quiet tears. Just as God sustained these couples in their uncertainty, He strengthened us in our own season of loss.

For Marty and I personally, our perseverance in love helped us honor one another. It helped us protect one another. It helped us not give up on each other. The season of my hysterectomy could have turned us against each other. I could have withdrawn in shame; Marty could have grown resentful or confused. Instead, in the middle of loss, he fed my faith, I wrestled honestly with God, and together we chose not to give up on emotional and spiritual intimacy while my body and identity were changing. That is what perseverance looked like for us in that valley.

The Double Rainbow Impasse

Perseverance doesn't happen in only one valley. Sometimes it returns in entirely different seasons, asking us to choose love all over again.

When we hit that marital impasse years ago—when divorce felt like the only emotionally honest option—we loaded the kids in the car and drove through a storm, both outside and inside. The double rainbow we saw that weekend didn't magically fix our problems, but it marked a turning point: we decided not to quit. We chose patience, prayer, and pastoral counseling instead of walking away. Looking back, perseverance looked like a van full of tears, a hotel room prayer, and a God who met us in our almost-ending. Couples often think perseverance will feel heroic.

Most of the time, it looks like two exhausted people choosing to drive toward help instead of away from each other.

The Pleurisy / Job Phone Call Story

Previously this story illustrated fighting for a spouse's faith. Now, let's examine it in the light of not giving up on praise during fear. Sometimes God gives previews of His faithfulness to keep us going. When Marty was flat on his back with pleurisy and I was sick with morning sickness, it would have been easy to let despair define that season. Instead, we chose to praise in the middle of fear. That was a tiny act of perseverance—holding on to worship when our circumstances screamed otherwise. God responded with a job offer and healing, but even if He had not, that choice to keep praising would still have been worth it. It taught us, early in marriage, how to hold on to God and each other when everything felt fragile.

My Birth Mother

Some valleys stretch so long that perseverance becomes the work of years instead of moments. Some wounds require the kind of endurance that keeps circling the same pain until healing finally breaks through.

As I mentioned earlier in this guide, making peace with my birth mother took years. I had to persevere toward wholeness and not give up on healing. It took decades for me to reach the moment when I collapsed at her feet and heard her whisper, "All is forgiven." For years, I carried resentment, confusion, and anger that seeped into my marriage. Perseverance in that part of my story did not look pretty. It looked like wrestling with God, circling the same pain over and over, and letting Marty gently point me back to grace.

When I finally made peace with my past, it didn't erase the trauma—but it freed our marriage from having to carry all of it. Sometimes, perseverance is simply refusing to stop pursuing healing, even when it feels like you're making no progress at all.

Remember What Made You Fall in Love

Perseverance doesn't just carry us through the hardest places—it also reminds us of the beauty worth fighting for. To keep going in marriage when it would be easier to stop, I borrow a technique from our daughter. She likes to remember what made her fall in love with our son-in-law when they were dating. They were next to a store in the mall. She asked him to wait on a bench outside the store for a few minutes while she finished her shopping. When she returned, she found him talking to a man whom our son-in-law introduced as his friend that they'd be taking to church the next day. When our daughter asked how long the two of them had known each other, our son-in-law told her five minutes. Our daughter fell in love with someone who could talk with ease to a complete stranger about God.

Decades earlier, my babysitter said, "Marry a man with a tremendous heart for our faithful God. There may be times you want to throw in the towel, but remembering what first caused you to fall in love, his heart, makes it easier to keep fighting for your marriage."

When the Halo Becomes a Crown

Around the time of our daughter's high school graduation, she entered a pageant. I am the exact opposite of a pageant mom, but I supported her desire to try for college support. When they announced that she had won, they placed a glistening silver tiara on her head. Her face said it all. The feeling was incomparable.

Just think. Instead of a sarcastic halo resting on your brow, someday you'll have a sincere crown of righteousness placed on your head. The feeling will be incomparable because for so long you've waited for a crown to toss at the feet of the Author of marriage. That is the very hope that makes the struggles so worthwhile. The sarcastic halo, all the years of struggle, misperception, and fatigue, becomes a crown of righteousness, the reward of having persevered in love and faith.

Summary

Perseverance is the quiet but unbreakable strength of love. It is choosing, again and again, to stay faithful, stay hopeful, and stay connected even when the path grows steep. Throughout Scripture and throughout our own marriage, we see that perseverance is not glamorous. It is not loud. It is built in the ordinary, painful, joyful, messy moments where love is tested.

Hannah persevered in prayer through years of disappointment; Job persevered in faith when his wife could not. Joseph and Mary persevered through relocation and danger, remaining obedient when the way was unclear. These stories teach us that endurance is a partnership between our obedience and God's sustaining grace.

In our own marriage, perseverance showed up in hospital rooms, financial strain, identity loss, emotional wounds from childhood, skunk-sprayed dogs, and seasons of unanswered prayer. Every time, God handed us the strength to help straighten each other's halos instead of allowing them to fall off completely. Perseverance is never about perfection—it is about choosing to keep walking toward God and toward each other when quitting might look easier.

And one day, when this life is finished and all the storms have passed, the halo we fought to keep steady will be replaced with a crown of righteousness—Jesus' reward for those who refused to give up. Until then, perseverance is the daily declaration that love never fails because God never fails those who cling to Him.

Chapter 13 Questions:

Reflect on the perseverance you have demonstrated in your marriage. Use the space provided to capture your thoughts. Discuss them with your spouse if you both agree.

When you read "love never gives up," what emotions or memories rise to the surface for you?

How do you personally define perseverance in marriage? Has that definition changed over the years?

Which part of perseverance is hardest for you—showing up, staying hopeful, or trusting God's timing?

Think of a recent challenge you and your spouse faced. How did each of you respond?

What helps your spouse persevere when life gets tough? What helps you persevere?

Where do you see progress in your marriage that came only through not giving up?

In what ways do you and your spouse help straighten each other's halos—lifting, calming, encouraging—when one of you is discouraged?

Are there wounds from your past that make perseverance in marriage more difficult?

Which biblical example from this chapter (Ruth, Hannah, Job, David) resonates most with your emotional story, and why?

How can you show perseverance in your healing journey without ignoring your limits or boundaries?

What does "holding hope for each other" look like in your marriage, especially when one spouse is struggling more than the other?

Which prayers have you been tempted to give up on?

How does worship—in the waiting or the silence—strengthen your perseverance?

How would your marriage change if you and your spouse committed to praying together, even briefly, every day?

Think of a "skunk spray" moment—something stressful that later became a funny story. What does that tell you about how God carries you through hard seasons?

Where is God inviting you to rediscover joy, laughter, or relief in this season?

How can joy act as a signpost that perseverance is working?

What "halo-tilting moments" in your marriage have ultimately strengthened your faith or compassion?

How does the promise of a crown of righteousness encourage you to keep going?

What daily choices can you make this week that say, "Love never gives up"?

Trauma Awareness: Perseverance

Perseverance is the quiet faith that refuses to let trauma have the final word. In a marriage touched by pain, it is the daily decision to stay present, to keep praying, and to keep believing that healing is possible. When life feels heavy and patterns of the past seem to repeat themselves, perseverance becomes the bridge between faith and fulfillment. It is love's way of saying, "Even here, I will not give up."

Trauma can make perseverance feel exhausting. The survivor may battle deep fatigue from years of emotional survival. The supporting spouse may grow weary from waiting, hoping, and trying to understand what cannot always be explained. In those moments, God's Word becomes a lifeline. "Let us run with endurance the race God has set before us. We do this by keeping our eyes on Jesus, the champion who initiates and perfects our faith." (Hebrews 12:1–2) Perseverance is not about pushing harder but looking higher. It means anchoring your marriage in God's strength rather than your own.

Healing from trauma is not linear. It is full of progress and setback, courage, and retreat. Couples who persevere learn that every step forward, no matter how small, matters to God. Romans 5:3–4 reminds us that endurance builds strength of character, and character strengthens confident hope. When we hold fast in faith, God shapes us through the waiting. Perseverance teaches us to see progress not only in what changes, but in what remains: our commitment, our prayers, and our trust in Him.

True perseverance also means extending grace when growth is slow. It means recognizing that both spouses are learning to love beyond comfort and to trust beyond understanding. It is the ability to look at the marriage not as a perfect story, but as a living testimony of God's faithfulness being written one choice at a time. Perseverance becomes a declaration of faith that love will not stop showing up.

Tool 1: The Long-Haul Plan

This tool helps couples develop a shared vision for endurance through long seasons of challenge or recovery.

- Name the Season – Identify what you are currently enduring together. Is it a healing process, a financial strain, a health challenge, or emotional distance? Naming it helps you face it as a team.

- Clarify What You Can Control – Write down what each of you can do to bring peace or stability to this season. For example: praying together nightly, seeking counseling, or managing household stress differently.

- Release What You Cannot Control – Pray together and give those burdens to God. Speak them aloud as you surrender them.

- Set Faith Goals – Agree on two or three goals that align with trust, patience, and grace rather than perfection.

This practice builds unity and shifts your focus to faith and hope for the future.

Tool 2: The Gratitude Reframe

- When discouragement sets in, gratitude reminds you of what still stands strong.

- When you feel hopeless, pause and name one thing that is still good today.

- Speak that gratitude out loud to your spouse or write it down.

- End your prayer by thanking God for His continued work, even when the full picture is not clear.

Gratitude softens the edges of exhaustion and redirects the heart toward endurance.

Exercise 1: The Faith Mile

Choose a physical or symbolic "mile" to walk together this week. It could be a walk around the block, a quiet evening drive, or a conversation without distraction. During this time, reflect on the miles you have already walked as a couple. End the time in prayer, thanking God for His hand on every step of your journey.

Exercise 2: Vows of Perseverance

Individually write a short paragraph beginning with the phrase, "I will keep showing up because…"

Write from the heart about what perseverance means in your marriage today. Read your paragraphs aloud to one another and place them somewhere visible. These vows serve as a reminder that love does not quit—it commits daily, even in silence and struggle.

Trauma Support Application

Perseverance for you may mean holding steady when your spouse's emotions feel unpredictable or when hope feels dim. You are not responsible for healing what you did not break, but you are called to stand beside your partner in faith. Your quiet consistency, gentle tone, and faith-filled words are what tell your spouse, "You are not alone in this."

When exhaustion tempts you to withdraw, return to God's promise in Isaiah 40:31: "But those who trust in the Lord will find new strength. They will soar high on wings like eagles. They will run and not grow weary. They will walk and not faint." Perseverance does not mean doing everything perfectly; it means depending on God's strength when yours is gone.

Show your spouse that love is still here in the simple things. Keep your word. Offer a prayer. Leave a note of encouragement. Be the calm presence that points them back to safety and faith.

Conclusion: Halos and Healing – Loving Through It All

I pray this guide has blessed you. Marty and I still have our sarcastic, tilted-halo moments, but they are the exception instead of the rule. As you have seen, references to the halo have been made and how the halo manifests in the actions demonstrated in the personal or Biblical stories. My own examples of trauma triggers have been included to further this demonstration. To recap, the following traits of love form a blueprint for a marriage founded in the nature of God. These principles teach us first and foremost that love is the answer to the questions, and God is love.

Love is patient. It doesn't allow its halo to tilt to sarcastically compare itself with the spouse. Love doesn't wound. It has compassion for the spouse still healing and sensitivity to the triggers of past wounds that come with marriage. It waits on the spouse and on God to respond.

Love is kind. A tilted halo would have love be critical of the spouse, but its straightened halo affirms the spouse. This love shows gratitude instead of entitlement, and compassion that protects and provides.

Love does not envy. A tilted halo would have love be jealous and resentful, but its straightened halo sees the spouse's blessings as victories for the marriage.

Love is not proud. A tilted halo would have love choose to win arguments and prove its worth, but its straightened halo acknowledges God's grace and readiness to forgive. This love readily forgives the spouse.

Love shows mutual respect. A tilted halo would have love seek its own way, but its straightened halo is considerate of the spouse above itself. This love commits to fulfill its responsibilities in marriage to grow into the person God desires.

Love honors by lifting each other up. While a tilted halo would have love manipulate the spouse with pride, selfishness, or careless words, its straightened halo practices humility, sacrifice, and respect, reflecting God's design for marriage.

Love finds joy in putting us before me. It lays aside its own preferences for unity. This love draws strength from a faith-filled community around it. While its tilted halo of self-absorption would have it sabotage intimacy and faith, its straightened halo sees the best in the spouse, continually works toward closeness, and encourages the spouse's faith.

Love has a calm spirit, responding instead of reacting. A tilted halo would have it say things it doesn't mean and recite the spouse's record of wrongs, but its straightened halo practices calmness and buries past wrongs. What begins as a small disagreement is blown completely out of proportion when a calm spirit is lacking.

Love forgives and clears the ledger. While a tilted halo would have it believe it doesn't need to forgive the spouse because of past trauma, its straightened halo allows God to birth forgiveness in the heart. Boundaries protect the heart, and prayer renews commitment to God and to each other.

Love has integrity. A tilted halo would have it believe it has a right to its skepticism of and isolation from a dishonest world, but its straightened halo humbles itself before God to accurately receive what the world needs to hear. Secrets grow in the dark until they destroy the very thing they were meant to protect. This love thrives on transparency.

Love protects and creates a safe haven. While a tilted halo would feel justified in sparse, insincere communication of love, its straightened halo commits to regular and genuine communication of love. This love removes harmful distractions and misguided affection.

Love trusts and hopes. It anchors in God's faithfulness. A tilted halo would have love irrationally harden its heart with harshness and cruelty, but its straightened halo exhibits steady wisdom, graciousness, generosity, and humility. This love leans on God instead of its own understanding, and reminds us that He is still writing our story when we can't see the ending.

Love perseveres. It holds on when it's hard. It chooses to keep straightening rather than discarding the spouse's halo when it tilts. It does this to bring it into the alignment of Christlike love. It keeps walking toward God and the spouse when quitting might look easier.

This book has been about celebrating how we choose love daily in the small acts of love, the consistency we show our spouse, and the support and the grace that we offer each other daily. The lessons in the chapters were meant to build cumulative habits that remind us that God is faithful, He is transformative, He is our anchor of Trust, Hope and Perseverance as the best example that Love does not give up as God never gives up on us.

The trauma awareness exercises were meant to build safety for healing to start together and with God. Spouses are partners, not adversaries or competitors. Both survivors and supporters need grace.

I pray you, both wives and husbands, will take hold of how dearly loved you are, enough that Jesus gave His life for you. Wives, I pray that you recognize your husband as head of the home just as Christ is head of the church. Husbands, I pray that you love your wife as Christ loved the church and gave Himself for her. Proverbs 18:22 says, "The man who finds a wife finds a treasure, and he receives favor from the Lord."

This is referring to a wife as described in this guide. God wouldn't give the husband His stamp of approval otherwise. We all have a part to play in working for the kingdom of God. We have a crown of righteousness awaiting us as our reward, but we have to make the shift from the tilted halo to our alignment to the crown.

The struggles you face are God's etchings on your heart to bring to the forefront of your realization who He is and what He can do. It seems like the enormous crystal punch bowl of your marriage slipped from your hands and hit the cement with such force that it sent shards flying in all directions. As God gets His whisk broom and dustpan, He asks you to let Him sweep it all up, and you oblige. He pours fresh cement, dumps the shards therein, and smooths them with His trowel. As the sun emerges from the clouds to shine on the crystal shards, it is apparent that a brilliant masterpiece has been created, catching the eye of the next struggling couple.

That, my friends, is what a Christian marriage is all about.

Thanks you for joining this journey with us.

Scan the QR code below for a blessing.

Numbers 6:24-26

About the Author

Sandy Haney grew up in sunny San Diego, California, surrounded by carefree beach life, though her own childhood was far from carefree. Through every hardship, her Christian faith became her anchor and source of strength. A retired teacher, Sandy now writes and speaks with compassion, helping others discover God's purpose in their seasons of pain. She and her husband of forty-four years make their home in the Texas Panhandle, where they delight in faith, family, and spoiling their grandchildren.

Made in the USA
Coppell, TX
20 January 2026